ENTERTAINING
D·E·S·S·E·R·T·S

TO HAL,
who had the idea and made it happen

ENTERTAINING
D·E·S·S·E·R·T·S

BY DEIRDRE PIRIE

PHOTOGRAPHS BY LOUIS WALLACH

◆

HOUGHTON MIFFLIN COMPANY

BOSTON   NEW YORK   LONDON   MELBOURNE   TORONTO

1991

For information about permission
to reproduce selections from this book,
write to Permissions,
Houghton Mifflin Company, 2 Park Street,
Boston, Massachusetts 02108.

Library of Congress Cataloging-in-Publication Data

Pirie, Deirdre
Entertaining desserts / by Deirdre Pirie ; photographs by Louis
Wallach.
p.   cm.
Includes index.
ISBN 0-395-55744-5
1. Desserts.   I. Title.
TX773.P575   1991
641.8'6—dc20   90-28910
CIP

Prepared and produced by
Chanticleer Press, New York

ACKNOWLEDGMENTS

As in all cookbooks, special thanks are due to many people. In this case my debt is largely to my mother, who not only was my inspiration but also gave my family wonderful and varied food and an interest in cooking and eating. My husband has been enthusiastic, but always a good critic. Our children have given invaluable assistance: Sophie has spent many hours reading and correcting the manuscript; John and Amanda have encouraged and tasted. Pauline Pollard has coped with the aftermath of a messy cook for more than twenty-five years.

The book would not have been completed without the help of my editors at Houghton Mifflin and Chanticleer Press, particularly Marge Berube and Ann ffolliott, who have shown such patience and fortitude.

The purpose of this book is to show that it is possible to fix fancy desserts at home, and that simple desserts can be made into elegant creations suitable for formal occasions. Although there are many fine pastry shops serving incredible treats, there are few restaurants that serve first-class dessert fare. Some restaurants seem to consider them an afterthought. Many customers are watching their waistlines and don't dare to have dessert. If instead they watched their intake of cream sauces and high-calorie meats, they could enjoy dessert without guilt. Restaurants have many advantages over the home cook in producing complex entrees and sauces. This is not true of desserts, and, with practice, the amateur can easily outdo the restaurant.

This cookbook is the result of an annual dessert party I have held for the last twenty years (see pages 206–207). At these parties, nothing is served but champagne and sweets. They are fun to cook for, since much can be prepared ahead, and without much help in advance it is entirely possible to "do it yourself" for one hundred or more people, if your house and your wishes permit.

I hope this book will provide inspiration to all, and that average cooks will find in it encouragement to pursue excellence and creativity.

CONTENTS

Opposite: Pear Sorbet (page 42)

INTRODUCTION

To most of us, dessert is the high point of the meal. To the cook, it is an expression of individuality and an opportunity to show off artistic accomplishments. Depending on the recipe, a great finale can be easy and quick or time-consuming and complicated. But with the exception of sugar artistry, most dessert-making techniques can be mastered with the use of a cookbook and a good sense of taste and design.

I have cooked in all types of kitchens. I grew up in a household in which my mother's first cook had been trained by my grandmother's cook, who had started as an apprentice — hardly allowed to touch the food — in the kitchen of the royal family in Vienna. My mother's cook went on to train her successor, who was the first professional cook I knew. Our cook disliked onlookers in the kitchen — especially children — and I was no exception, so I had to try to be unseen as well as unheard when I wished to observe. On Saturday mornings, I remember watching in awe as she made huge batches of dough for coffee cake, a heavy, sticky mixture requiring strenuous beating — by hand of course. I watched as she mixed doughs, almost never referring to a cookbook, and rolled thin pastry to encase plums or apples. On a good day, if she happened to make jelly doughnuts, I might be allowed to put the jelly in the middle of each. Years later, when my mother tried to decipher her cookbook, the recipe for doughnuts said, "Take flour, milk, an egg, yeast and some butter and make a nice dough as for bread." I was able to help my mother work out the proportions and techniques because I remembered how the doughs looked and tasted, and how they were rolled and cooked. There are no secrets from children!

During the Second World War, my mother started a restaurant in New York City called the Cordon Bleu. She knew little about cooking, but learned of necessity because the restaurant chef was often absent. At night the restaurant ran a cooking school that soon became a gathering place for celebrities and socialites wanting to learn "the gentle art." The practice mother gained there came in handy as the years went by, since she had to do without the luxury of a cook for long periods.

Unlike some of her cooks, my mother welcomed my assistance and together we used to experiment. When I was about seven, she decided I needed to know how to cook a few things and started me with hollandaise sauce, which by her recipe was tricky and would curdle if you blinked hard. I graduated to cookies. She let me riffle through her cookbooks and try any recipes that I could convince her might produce good cookies. I soon learned that flowery descriptions do not necessarily translate into delicious results, and that one can tell a lot about the ultimate taste by reading the ingredients, noting the proportions, and studying the directions. Soon I learned to comprehend how the cookie would taste. I copied recipes and collected them in a special book, always concentrating on desserts. One of the first, copied in a first-grade classroom in huge letters on ruled paper, was for ghastly sugar cookies with an artificially colored sugar glaze. My tastes have certainly changed.

When I became engaged, the man who was to become my husband was wooed with sweets. His student kitchen was equipped with a sort of griddle, with a space underneath in which one could broil or "bake." Baking in it was a real trick, since there was no source of heat on the bottom. Always ambitious, I started by making cookies and then soufflés — both items not receptive to being broiled. But I learned to make elaborate tents of aluminum foil to deflect the heat and had amazingly good results. In fact, when we were married and had a real kitchen, many of my soufflés failed. It took time to adjust to a proper oven.

Cooking on a wood-fired mountain stove, over an open fire, and on a boat stove fueled with alcohol have taught me adaptability. Chocolate chip cookies baked in a tiny oven at 10,000 feet were exceedingly popular, and homemade pasta and bread on a sailboat, although not difficult, were considered by others to be great feats. While this book presupposes a modern kitchen with time-saving gadgets, all the recipes can be done by hand, with time and patience. A good oven is the only essential appliance.

Through the years, I have often enjoyed the challenge of trying something ridiculously hard, when the result in no way justified the work. For this book, however, I have selected recipes in which the end justifies the effort involved. Otherwise, this is a personal collection of dessert recipes. Many are family heirlooms; others are well-known classics that can be used as starting points for personal innovations. Some are adaptations to the lighter style of cooking favored in the last few years. Although these recipes are designed to be made by a cook who must also play host or hostess, this does not mean that the desserts can all be prepared ahead and left waiting. I have found that, warnings of Emily Post to the contrary, my guests are quite tolerant of my leaving the table for a few minutes to put the finishing touches on a grand finale. Sometimes the disruption and anticipation are more than compensated for by the aesthetic appeal of blue and orange flames leaping from a flambéed dessert, or the lightness of a soufflé that remains elegantly puffed, or the taste sensation of hot-and-cold mixtures that have not melded to an insipid lukewarm.

Frequently a cook is warned not to try new recipes on guests for fear of failure. But few of us have the time or the figures to take that warning seriously. Who really wants to make a croquembouche for a small family lunch? But desserts can be categorized by technique, and you can master the basic technique in each category before experimenting in public with more difficult versions. For instance, plain cream puffs — the heart of a croquembouche — can be made for a simple gathering. After that it is easy enough to do the other time-consuming, but not so difficult, steps to make the more elaborate dessert when the occasion demands it.

Learn to read the recipes, and recognize the procedures that are familiar and those that may require practice. For cooks, reading recipes is similar to how musicians read sheet music: Accomplished musicians can hear the music when they read it and they understand the difficulties involved in producing it. Cooks must be able to visualize the whole process and imagine the taste, textures, and appearance of the final product. With time, you will develop the ability to create new variations even without entering the kitchen, by using recipes as inspiration rather than as formulas. Creating your own artistic triumphs is what makes cooking fun, and it is the spirit to which this book is dedicated.

NOTES AND TECHNIQUES

Baking Where you place things in your oven can be critical. Cakes need generous space around, above, and below them for even rising. Where possible, the layers should be put on the same shelf in alternate corners in the middle of the oven. They should not be moved during the first three-quarters of the cooking time as they will fall. The same is even more true of soufflés, which are highly allergic to any draft of cooler air.

Blind cooked tarts, those that are precooked and filled later, should be placed near the bottom of the oven, because their rims tend to brown too much if they are near the top. They are not so fussy about drafts and can be moved midway through baking.

Slip a piece of aluminum foil loosely over the top of a cake or pastry if the top browns too quickly.

Brownies and other bar cookies have a tendency to dry out along the edges. You can avoid this by using insulation strips (available from cooking specialty shops) placed on the outside of the pan, or by putting a strip of doubled aluminum foil around the edge. When recipes are doubled and a larger pan is used, cut the temperature down about a fifth and bake longer.

Cookies can be moved around and in most ovens baking sheets need to be reversed for even cooking. If you cook three trays at once, you will surely have to move them around, top to bottom and front to back. Some baking sheets are double thick, with a layer of air between the layers of tin. They are excellent for use in electric ovens, but most gas ovens do not require them.

Timing is a matter of knowing the properties of the oven you are using. Electric ovens cool faster, because they have no pilot lights. They also tend to produce a very hot spot near the bottom. Note that all times given in this book are somewhat approximate.

Cakes should be tested with a broom straw or, if you are so inclined, with a wire tester designed for the purpose. I prefer the straw snatched from a real straw (not synthetic) broom, even though it may be less sanitary, because it is less slippery and the dough clings to it better. For most cakes, the straw should come out slightly damp, with very few crumbs adhering to it. For brownies, the straw should be very moist and the crumbs adhering to it can be tested for doneness. Soufflés should on no account be punctured. Savarins should be pressed with your finger, and are done when they feel hard and quite hot.

Berries In general, never wash berries if at all possible. You should never wash raspberries under any circumstances, because they will turn to mush. Strawberries may be washed very carefully as follows. Fill a large pot with cold water. Put berries in a colander and immerse it in water, shaking gently. Immediately drain berries and spread them out on a dish towel. Take the edge of the towel in your hands and gently roll the berries around on it to absorb the water, or pat them dry gently with a second towel. This should be done just before serving.

Adding sugar to berries will cause them to release their juices. If they are to be strained, it is wise to put the sugar on several hours in advance. Sugar will also stop them from getting moldy so quickly, so if berries must be kept several days it is often wise to cover them completely with granulated sugar.

Mold is a problem when storing berries. Before putting berries in the refrigerator, lay them on a plate or baking sheet in a single layer. Never leave them covered with plastic wrap.

Butter Almost all pastry chef recipes call for sweet (unsalted) butter. Many recipes then specify adding salt. When I have specified butter, I mean salted butter. If you use sweet butter, you may wish to add salt. In any case, use a good brand of butter, because cheaper ones often contain more water, and when melted, may have less butterfat. In my opinion, sweet butter is not worth the extra amount of money it costs. In certain recipes that call for a great deal of butter, or where the flavor of the butter really stands out, I have specified sweet butter.

Homemade butter is favored by some cooks, but it must be used with discretion and tends to be somewhat watery, depending on how carefully it was made.

Chocolate Chocolate is perhaps the single most important ingredient beside sugar in many dessert recipes. For the recipes in this book, when I call for unsweetened chocolate, I usually use Baker's, since most other unsweetened chocolates are hard to find. When I call for semisweet chocolate, you can use any ordinary cooking chocolate such as Maillard Eagle Sweet, Baker's semisweet or Baker's German's Sweet. Many imported varieties are higher in quality but can be difficult to find. For glazes and decorations, it is best to use a good quality of *couverture* chocolate. It is available in large bars from various gourmet catalogs and will keep for several years. White chocolate does not keep well, so buy in small quantities. Milk chocolate is uncommon in desserts, and none is called for in this book.

Never heat chocolate too quickly or too much. It should be kept under 120°F. Do not heat over simmering or boiling water, because the steam will cause the chocolate to seize up. If this occurs, add boiling water, tablespoon by tablespoon, until it can be stirred to smoothness. To heat chocolate to the right consistency, place it in a pan over boiling water and let it sit, off the heat, stirring from time to time. For recipes in which chocolate will be cooked, such as Chocolate Pots-de-Creme (page 18) or the chocolate sauces, you can be rather harsher in your treatment and use the microwave or melt it in a pan set directly on the flame.

Cream   In most cases, heavy cream is specified in these recipes. This term refers to what the dairy industry calls "heavy." In some stores, it is also referred to as "whipping cream." In any case, always attempt to get cream containing the highest butterfat obtainable and try to get cream that has no preservatives in it. Do not use crème fraîche as found in American stores. It is not the same as that found in Europe and will not melt well. Storebought cream should always be whipped when icy cold and it may be necessary to chill the beaters and bowl.

If you should happen to have access to a lovely Jersey cow, her product will bear no resemblance to the industry standard. Fresh farm cream comes in varying thicknesses and must be treated with great care. If properly cleaned containers and separator are used, it may be kept refrigerated without spoiling for as long as a month. It may also be frozen, but in that case it is primarily useful in dishes in which the cream is cooked. One or two tablespoons of such cream, fresh or frozen, can be added to storebought cream. The cream will gradually thicken to an acceptable consistency.

Farm cream should have all the milk separated from it either by a separator or by allowing it to settle and then spooning off the top. When freshly separated, farm cream is almost as thin as the storebought variety, but within a day it gets thicker and in several days you will be able to stand a spoon in the middle of it without the spoon falling over. Very heavy cream has to be used with care. When making ice cream and whipped cream, you should thin it with milk or it will turn to butter when whipped. To serve it at its best, whip it very slightly, add a tiny bit of sugar, and serve in a bowl with a gravy server. Do not ever attempt to whip it very stiff without adding milk first.

Egg Whites   One of the most important ingredients of many desserts, egg whites have to be handled with great care. They simply will not elevate properly if a trace of grease, moisture, or egg yolk is present. Always make sure your bowl is thoroughly dry. It is better not to dry it with a dish towel, which might contain traces of grease. When possible, keep a special bowl for beating egg whites and always wash and dry it in the dishwasher. (Ditto for the beater.) If you use a copper bowl, you will achieve greater volume. Fine beaters with many wires are preferable to coarse ones. A half lemon can be rubbed on the bowl before beating egg whites if grease is suspected. Do not ever use a plastic bowl! I generally add a pinch of cream of tartar per egg white whether or not a recipe calls for it.

It is easier to achieve volume with egg whites that are warm (between 65–90°F) and at least 3 days old. Separated egg whites may be kept in tightly covered glass jars in the refrigerator for several days, or even for a couple of weeks if they came fresh from the chicken and not the supermarket.

Many desserts can be made less fattening and lighter if you use beaten egg whites in addition to or instead of part of the whipped cream called for in the recipe. Try this when making the Raspberry Bavarian Cream Carême (page 27) or Maple Mousse (page 29).

Folding In This term is used often, and is a key technique in the making of successful desserts. Most often you will be required to fold a light air-filled mixture, such as whipped cream or egg white, into a heavier base. The base should always be at the bottom and the lighter mixture placed on top. It is a good practice to place only a third or less of the light mixture on top to start with. When that is thoroughly incorporated, the rest can be folded into the now somewhat lighter and more flexible base.

I usually use a long-handled rubber spatula and bring the spatula down through the 2 mixtures, carrying some of the light mixture down to the bottom. Keeping the spatula near the edge of the bowl, I come up on the opposite side, bringing the lower mixture to the surface. Repeat this process until a somewhat even texture is achieved. Do not strive to remove all traces of the egg white or cream; if you persist you will lose too much of the valuable air you have incorporated. Beware of losing total volume. Experience will soon tell you when enough is enough.

Salt In most of my recipes, salt is optional. Where butter is called for, I generally use regular butter, which contains a great deal of salt. More is unnecessary unless the dessert tastes too bland. If a recipe seems too salty, use sweet butter to replace the normal salted variety. A small touch of salt does wonders for fruit dishes, such as the Fresh Fruit Compote (page 142), and can act as a replacement for sugar. It is also useful in plain white cakes, such as that used for Coconut Snowballs (page 53), and in meringues and boiled frostings.

CHAPTER 1

MOUSSES AND CREAM MIXTURES

Chestnut Mont Blanc (page 16)

Mousses, chilled or frozen desserts normally based on whipped cream, are excellent do-ahead desserts. While giving the impression of lightness after a heavy meal, they are in fact highly caloric and rich unless some or all of the cream is replaced with beaten egg white. Mousses cannot be molded easily unless they are frozen. This differentiates them from Bavarian Creams, which contain gelatin and are stiff enough to hold their shape after normal refrigeration. If you wish to make a splendid, decorated dessert, make a frozen mousse or a Bavarian Cream in a fancy mold and decorate it. These desserts can really show artistic talents and will produce a fantastic finale. Mousses are also classic, but are not as easy to work with.

Exact proportions are not critical in the recipes, and the cook should feel free to substitute some well-beaten egg white for cream if calories or cholesterol are important concerns. However, beaten egg whites do not freeze well, so it is best to use a cooked meringue or just use whipped cream in frozen mousses.

When making mousses, be sure that the flavor mixture is first lightened by thoroughly stirring in a third of the beaten egg white or whipped cream before attempting to fold in the remainder. It is impossible to fold a light mixture into something heavy or sticky without losing excessive volume.

◆
◆
◆

CHESTNUT MONT · BLANC

Chestnuts provide a wonderfully different taste and texture for desserts, although not everyone likes their flavor. Preparing fresh chestnuts is a lot of work; imported chestnuts bottled in heavy syrup, although very expensive, make an acceptable substitute, as do canned pureed chestnuts. If you use preserved chestnuts, omit making the syrup — use that included in the jar. Pureed chestnuts are already sweetened.

Aesthetically, this is a very pleasing dessert if you take the time to present it as suggested (see photograph on page 15). Be sure the cream in the center is put through a pastry bag with a decorating tube on the end.

This dessert is also nice served on a plate of Vanilla Custard Sauce (page 175), marbleized with a chocolate sauce. Pass the extra sauce separately.

1 cup milk
1 inch vanilla bean
1 pound chestnuts in shells, or
    12-ounce jar preserved chestnuts
⅔ cup sugar
¼ cup water
1 tablespoon butter
Crème Chantilly (page 175)

1. Scald milk, add vanilla bean, and set aside.

2. If using fresh chestnuts, with a sharp knife, cut slits in chestnut shells. Place them in a saucepan, cover with cold water, and bring to a boil. Remove pan from burner and take one chestnut from pan at a time, remove the shell, and place in scalded milk. If using preserved chestnuts, add to milk. When last chestnut has been added, bring milk to a boil. Remove, rinse, and set aside vanilla bean, then rub chestnuts and milk through a sieve or potato ricer.

3. In a heavy saucepan, simmer sugar, water, and reserved vanilla bean to make a syrup, about 5 minutes. Cook syrup until it reaches 235°F., or forms a soft ball when dropped in cold water. Remove vanilla bean, slit it, and scrape seeds back into syrup. Blend syrup with chestnut milk and work mixture very thoroughly until it forms a thick paste. (A food processor removes the drudgery here.) Cool to lukewarm and stir in butter.

4. Fill a pastry bag with chestnut mixture and force it through a ⅛-inch round nozzle, letting it fall at random onto a buttered and sugared 1-quart ring mold, or force the mixture through a potato ricer or food mill. A light touch is needed to obtain a nestlike effect. Do not pack mixture in tightly. Carefully unmold still-warm chestnut mold onto a chilled platter and chill for 2 hours. Fill center with a dome of Crème Chantilly piped through a pastry bag.

Working time: 2 hours (or 1 hour if preserved chestnuts are used)
Preparation time: 4 hours
Serves 10–12

◆

CHOCOLATE POTS-DE-CRÈME

This is a wonderful dish to have waiting for children returning from college or school. It is simple to make if you are careful to cook the egg mixture over low heat. It keeps for several days in the refrigerator, although the top will form a thin skin. Made with very thick, unpasteurized cream from a good Jersey cow, it achieves a trufflelike consistency of incredible smoothness and is so rich that even confirmed chocolate lovers have trouble finishing more than one. With store-bought cream, it is less rich but still delicious.

6 ounces semisweet chocolate
2 cups heavy cream
4 egg yolks

1. In a heavy saucepan, boil chocolate and cream, stirring constantly until thick and smooth.

2. Put chocolate mixture in a food processor. As food processor is running, add egg yolks, one at a time. The mixture should be very thick.

(It may be necessary to put mixture in a double boiler over hot water and cook very carefully until thick as soft custard.)

3. Fill demitasse cups or pots-de-crème dishes and refrigerate for several hours.

N O T E : You may use any brand of good-quality sweet or semisweet chocolate, but don't substitute unsweetened or milk chocolate.

Working time: 20 minutes
Preparation time: 4 hours
Serves 6

◆

WARM CHOCOLATE MOUSSES

This dessert has the texture of a tart, the ingredients of a soufflé, and it looks like a pudding. The trick is to serve the mousse hot and the sorbet cold. Use the best-quality chocolate. The centers should be soft and somewhat runny, and the outside should be crusty — rather like a hot soufflé.

4 ounces semisweet, Maillard Sweet, or other imported chocolate

1½ ounces unsweetened chocolate

10 tablespoons butter, at room temperature

3 eggs

½ cup sugar

½ cup plus 2 teaspoons flour

1½ tablespoons cocoa powder, preferably imported

¾ teaspoon baking powder

2 cups Fruit Sorbet (page 42) or Pear Coulis (page 154)

2 cups vanilla ice cream or whipped cream

1. Place 6 sheets of parchment paper on baking sheet or cover baking sheet with heavy-duty aluminum foil well coated with nonstick spray. Place 6 small tart or English muffin rings on parchment paper or foil.

2. Melt chocolate and butter in a double boiler over hot water, and remove from heat.

3. Beat eggs, adding sugar, flour, cocoa, and baking powder. Add to chocolate and stir well with a whisk.

4. Fill rings half-full, and freeze for at least 3 hours, or up to several days.

5. While they are still frozen, bake mousses at 375°F. for about 12 minutes, until just starting to get firm. The centers should remain damp and shiny. Allow to cool slightly, about 2 to 3 minutes.

6. Cut rings away from mousses with a small, sharp knife, and remove rings. Cut paper between them. Flip each upside-down on a plate and carefully peel off paper.

7. Garnish each mousse with a scoop of sorbet or coulis and a dollop of whipped cream or ice cream.

Working time: 1 hour
Preparation time: 2 hours
Serves 6

◆

CRÈME BRÛLÉE

When prepared correctly, this classic dessert is worth its astounding number of calories. The total depth of the custard should be kept to a minimum so that each bite is accompanied by sufficient crunchy topping. In recent years, Crème Brûlée has enjoyed a return to popularity, but the custard is sometimes flavored with fruit, herbs, or chocolate. I prefer the classic version.

4 cups heavy cream
8 egg yolks
1 tablespoon granulated sugar
⅛ teaspoon salt
1 to 2 cups brown sugar, packed
 (See Note)

1. Heat cream to boiling point in top of a double boiler. Pour immediately into a food processor and turn processor on high.

2. Add egg yolks, granulated sugar, and salt. Process for 1 minute, then return mixture to double boiler. Cook over hot water, stirring constantly with a wooden spoon, until mixture is thick and coats the spoon, about 5 to 10 minutes. Do not allow custard to get too hot or it will curdle.

3. Place custard in a shallow broiler-proof 2-quart dish — one that is not made of metal or any material that conducts heat quickly — or in 8 in-dividual soufflé dishes. The mixture should be 1½ inches deep or less. Refrigerate at least 1 hour, or until very cold. The custard should set and be firm on top while remaining soft underneath.

4. Preheat broiler, and place custard dish in a larger baking pan, at least as deep as the dish. Fill baking pan with ice cubes and a little water. Make sure the ice water reaches top of the custard line or higher. Using a coarse strainer and with the back of a spoon, rub brown sugar through it over the custard, being sure to cover surface totally.

5. Place custard dish under broiler and broil until sugar is melted and very glassy, about 3 minutes. Remove from broiler at once, and let sit for about 3 minutes, until dish cools. Repeat brown sugar, broiling, and cooling steps 3 or 4 times, until you have built up a nice thick layer of amber candy that will take a hard crack of a spoon to break.

6. Serve at once. Do not put back in refrigerator or it will get sugary. If dessert must wait, leave it in the pan of ice water to keep cool.

NOTE: You can use either light or dark brown sugar, depending on the strength of flavor you prefer. The custard can be made firmer by adding an extra egg yolk or two, but the Crème Brûlée tastes best when the custard is quite soft.

Working time: 1 hour
Preparation time: 2 hours
Serves 8

Opposite: Crème Brûlée

◆

APRICOT MOUSSE

The ingredients for this recipe are always on hand in my house, ready for unexpected company. Prunes and apricots will keep in the refrigerator for up to 6 months. This mousse is very good when served in Chocolate Crinkle Cups (page 199), Sand Tarts (page 100), or as the filling for the Apricot Meringue Torte (page 115).

In a pinch you can use apricot jam instead of dried apricots and sugar, but omit the cooking. Also, you can substitute prunes for apricots. Store-bought pitted prunes generally are of very high quality and will keep indefinitely if unopened.

For variation, use more cream and fewer egg whites to give the mousse a richer, creamier consistency.

1 cup boiling water
8 ounces dried apricots
½ cup sugar, approximately
3 egg whites
½ cup heavy cream (optional)
Chocolate Curls (page 200) (optional)

1. Pour boiling water over dried fruit and allow it to sit for 10 minutes. (If you are in a hurry, you can cook fruit on the stove until it boils.)

2. Puree fruit with most of its juice in a food processor. Add more liquid and, if necessary, additional water

to make mixture about as thick as cooked, cooled oatmeal.

3. Add ¼ cup sugar to apricot puree and taste. Apricots vary in sweetness, so add sugar accordingly. The mixture should be somewhat tart, since you will be adding sugar with egg whites. Let apricot puree cool to room temperature.

4. Beat egg whites until stiff, then gradually add remaining ¼ cup sugar, beating until very thick. If using cream, whip it.

5. Fold mixtures together. Pour mousse into a 1-quart serving bowl, then chill and top with Chocolate Curls or other decoration.

N O T E : If you are counting calories, you can substitute artificial sweetener for the sugar added to the apricots, added when the puree has cooled to lukewarm.

Working time: 15 minutes
Preparation time: 2 hours
Serves 6–10

◆

COEUR À LA CRÈME

This is an excellent choice for Valentine's Day or an outdoor lunch. It is normally eaten without a full complement of silverware, and it is a little crumbly and messy for a formal dinner. To eat it, place a small amount of cream on a slice of toast, top with a berry and a sprinkling of sugar, and eat like an open sandwich.

Coeur à la Crème molds are traditionally made of wicker, but heart-shaped porcelain ones are more readily available. They have many holes in the bottom through which the whey can drain.

1 pound cottage cheese
1 pound cream cheese, at room temperature

2 cups heavy cream
Baked Toast (recipe follows)

1. Rub cottage cheese through a fine

sieve or beat in a mixer. Do not use a food processor, which will make the cottage cheese watery.

2. Add cream cheese, mixing well, then slowly add heavy cream. Beat very well — mixture must be absolutely smooth without a sign of a lump. If it is not really smooth, rub through a fine strainer.

3. Line a 5- or 6-inch Coeur à la Crème basket or mold with cheese-cloth and fill, or place mixture in a cloth set in a colander, and mold it later. Set in refrigerator overnight to drain.

4. Surround Coeur with fresh strawberries and serve with toast and sugar on the side.

BAKED TOAST

¼ **pound sweet butter**
1 loaf bread, very thinly sliced

1. Preheat oven to 325°F.

2. Melt butter in a small pan. Do not brown.

3. Cut crusts off bread slices.

4. Lightly brush both sides of bread slices with melted butter and place on a baking sheet.

5. Bake until brown on the bottom, about 5 minutes. Turn over and bake until other side is light brown, another 5 minutes. Be careful not to overcook! Toast should be just tan.

N O T E : You can keep the toast in a tightly covered tin box for up to 24 hours, or freeze and reheat when needed. It is excellent served with soup or as a base for appetizers.

Working time: 30 minutes
Preparation time: 24 hours
Serves 10 – 12

◆

RASPBERRY BAVARIAN
CREAM CARÊME

When made with fresh raspberries, formed in a fancy mold, and decorated with fresh raspberries and piped whipped cream, this dessert will be as appealing to the eye as to the palate. The recipe is attributed to the great chef Antonin Carême (1783–1833), master of Talleyrand's kitchens for twelve years and cook to the royal families of England and Austria.

Straining the raspberries is the most difficult part of what is really a very simple recipe. You must use a very fine strainer, such as a *chinois,* to be certain that no specks of seed get in.

You need about 2 cups of puree for this recipe. I strain the berries in large batches and freeze some puree for future use. If you use frozen raspberries, omit the sugar and add lemon juice to taste.

1 quart fresh raspberries
¾ cup superfine sugar, approximately
2 tablespoons unflavored gelatin
¼ cup cold water
1 tablespoon fresh lemon juice
2 cups heavy cream

1. Place raspberries in a bowl. Pour sugar over them, and stir once or twice, then leave unrefrigerated for several hours. Berries will break down and release their juice.

2. Using a metal spoon, rub berry pulp against a fine strainer until only seeds are left.

3. Soften gelatin in a bowl with cold water, then place bowl over boiling water, stirring until gelatin is completely dissolved.

4. Combine raspberry puree and lemon juice with dissolved gelatin. Taste to be sure mixture is correctly sweetened. Add more sugar, if necessary. Stir in a bowl placed over ice water until mixture thickens slightly. Do not allow gelatin mixture to thicken too much or it will not accept whipped cream without lumping. (If gelatin mixture does harden, warm slightly and process in food processor, then immediately fold in whipped cream.)

5. Whip cream, and fold into raspberry mixture. Place in a 2½-quart mold, and chill for at least 4 hours.

NOTE: This dessert can be made up to 24 hours in advance, but if you use a tin-lined mold, the dessert must be unmolded after 5 hours or the chemical action between the acid in the raspberries and the tin will create purple stains on the dessert. If you use a plastic or other nonmetallic mold, you can leave it for up to 48 hours. After 48 hours, the cream may start to sour.

Working time: 1 hour
Preparation time: 4 hours
Serves 8–10

◆

RUM BAVARIAN CREAM

This is a wonderful Bavarian cream on its own, decorated with Chocolate Curls or Chocolate Leaves (pages 200, 201) or served with Thin Chocolate Sauce (page 179). It is the main ingredient of the Chocolate Surprise Package (page 160).

2½ tablespoons unflavored gelatin

3¾ cups milk

6 eggs, separated

1¼ cups sugar

¼ cup dark rum, preferably Myers's

¼ teaspoon cream of tartar

1 cup heavy cream, whipped

⅓ cup finely chopped pecans

¾ cup crushed almond macaroon crumbs

1. Sprinkle gelatin over 1 cup milk to soften.

2. Heat remaining milk in a double boiler to just below boiling. Add the softened gelatin and stir to blend.

3. In a medium bowl, beat egg yolks and ½ cup sugar; gradually add hot milk, being careful not to curdle.

4. Return mixture to top of a double boiler and cook over simmering water until custard coats a spoon, about 15 minutes. Remove from heat, cool, and add rum. Refrigerate, or stir over ice, until mixture is thick and mounds slightly when lifted with a spoon.

5. Beat egg whites with cream of tartar. Gradually add ¾ cup sugar, beating until stiff peaks are formed.

6. Fold together whipped cream, egg whites, and custard mixture, and turn it into a 2- to 2½-quart mold or large, round mixing bowl with the largest diameter the same as your cake pan, if you are making the Chocolate Surprise Package.

7. Mix nuts and macaroon crumbs, and spread over Bavarian Cream, pressing gently into surface. Refrigerate until ready to serve.

Working time: 30 minutes
Preparation time: 4 hours
Serves 12

◆

MAPLE MOUSSE

This delicious mousse makes a wonderful dessert to serve to visiting foreigners, many of whom have never experienced maple syrup. If caramelizing the sugar is too much trouble, use 1½ cups of maple syrup and no sugar.

This mousse can be made days ahead and frozen with minimal loss of taste if it is carefully wrapped. It should be brought to just above freezing for serving.

1 cup maple syrup

5 egg yolks, lightly beaten

⅛ teaspoon salt (optional)

1 cup sugar

1 cup chopped roasted almonds

1 teaspoon vanilla extract

4 cups heavy cream

Roasted slivered almonds or whipped cream, for decoration

1. Cook maple syrup with egg yolks over low heat or in a double boiler, stirring constantly, until syrup is thick as molasses, about 8 to 10 minutes. Add salt, if desired, and chill.

2. Caramelize sugar in a cast-iron frying pan, stirring constantly over medium heat until it turns a dark golden brown, about 5 minutes. Turn into a lightly buttered pan to cool.

3. When caramel is cold, pound into fine powder between 2 sheets of wax paper with a rolling pin, or grind in a food processor.

4. Combine maple custard, powdered caramelized sugar, almonds, and vanilla in a bowl.

5. Whip cream, and fold into mixture. Pour into a 1½-quart mold and freeze for 4 to 6 hours.

6. Unmold and decorate the top with slivered almonds to create a hedgehog effect, or with rosettes of whipped cream.

Working time: 40 minutes
Preparation time: 5 hours–overnight
Serves 8

◆

BERRY BRÛLÉE

This is an easy and impressive version of fruit with cream. A mixture of ½ whipped cream and ½ sour cream can be substituted for crème fraîche. Strawberries, blueberries, or other berries may be used if desired.

2 10-ounce packages frozen raspberries, or 4 cups fresh berries
1 cup crème fraîche
¼ cup light brown sugar, packed (approximately)

1. If using frozen raspberries, drain off juice. Divide berries among 4 broilerproof ramekins. Cover berries with crème fraîche and chill for at least 1 hour.

2. Just before serving, preheat broiler. Sieve brown sugar over cream-covered berries, then broil 4 inches from heat just until sugar melts. Serve without delay!

Working time: 10 minutes
Preparation time: 1½ hours
Serves 4

◆

CHAPTER 2

ICE CREAMS, SORBETS, AND ICES

Ice-Cream Bombe (page 38)

There are so many terms today for frozen dessert mixtures that it is easy to be confused. The somewhat arbitrary definitions that follow are mine and are shared by some, but certainly not all, sources. Ice cream is easy; most agree that it is a frozen mixture of cream, flavoring, and possibly egg and milk. But then so is frozen mousse. The difference is that a mousse is frozen without turning; it achieves its volume from beaten cream, whereas ice cream increases in volume from being beaten while freezing.

Sorbets, sherbets, ices, granités, spooms, frozen yogurts, and ice milks are all terms that appear with increasing frequency as consumers become more diet conscious. Ices are made of fruit juice or other flavored liquids like chocolate, coffee, or champagne, mixed with sugar and water and frozen in an ice-cream freezer. Granités are similar mixtures frozen without turning, resulting in a frozen dessert full of ice crystals, with a coarse texture. Spooms are sherbets with the addition of partially beaten egg whites. So then what are sherbets? The term is used for many frozen concoctions. Always frozen in an ice-cream freezer, they are made of fruit juice or other flavoring, sugar, water, and sometimes milk. They are very smooth and have more substance than ices.

Ice milk is a low-fat "ice cream." Frozen yogurt uses yogurt to replace the cream of conventional ice cream. That leaves sorbet. I simply cannot be sure what sorbet is and isn't. The recipes that exist for sorbet are indistinguishable from those that were formerly called ice and sherbet. But it's a nice sounding word, found on most of the menus of the eighties, so why not call these desserts by the new name?

TECHNIQUES AND SERVING TIPS

There are myriad ice-cream freezers on the market today. Some produce frozen mush directly from frozen fruit; others require a central can to be frozen, then the mixture is placed in it, turned a few times and produces "ice cream."

I am old-fashioned and prefer a traditional ice-cream freezer that employs lump ice and rock salt, and that takes 20 to 30 minutes to achieve results. The product is far lighter and smoother than that produced by its more up-to-date counterparts. Compromise if you wish, and be sure to follow the manufacturer's instructions. But if you want to use an old-fashioned freezer, here is what you do:

Put your well-chilled mixture in the metal central can, filling it no more than three-fourths full to allow for expansion. Place the can in the bucket, and put the motor in position or secure the crank. Fill all the space around the cylinder with ice, crushing some if necessary. Put in about 3 tablespoons of coarse salt (kosher or rock salt) for every 3 inches of ice. When the bucket is filled to within 3 inches of the top, finish with an additional layer of salt. Add water to come about halfway up the ice, so that the can will be in full contact with the cold. Replenish the salt and ice as they dissolve. Turn on the motor or begin cranking. Continue until the motor starts to labor or the crank is difficult to turn. At this point the ice cream should be ready. Don't over-turn. The ice cream is best stored in the can, surrounded with ice and an extra half cup of salt to further lower the temperature. Be careful not to let any salt water in when removing the lid and the paddle.

This method allows you to vary the freezing temperature for each mixture. The more salt you add, the colder the temperature of the ice water and the faster the mixture will freeze. This is good for very rich ice cream, where too much turning can result in butter. Sherbets get a smoother texture by being frozen more slowly at lower temperatures. If a sherbet mixture refuses to freeze, it may contain too little or too much sugar. The former stays watery and the latter gets syrupy, like jam.

Most restaurants today include sorbets on their menus. At some restaurants, sorbet is brought automatically after the main course to refresh the palate. When offered as a dessert, two or three varieties are frequently served together, usually three complementary flavors and colors. Chocolate, raspberry, and lime make a nice combination.

At home I use sorbets to set off a rich cake or a fancy cookie. At lunch in the summertime, sorbet with a bit of fresh fruit compote is nicer than just plain fruit. Unlike homemade ice cream, which has a tendency to get crystalline in just a few days, sorbets tend to keep quite well in the freezer. Ice cream made without egg yolks will store better than custard-based ice creams, but all taste best when freshly made.

Good quality plain vanilla ice cream served with hot fudge sauce may be mundane, but it is a truly great dessert. It can be embellished with decorations, meringue, praline, additional sauces, and cookies or cakes, but even in its plainest form it is attractive and delicious. Never overlook the commonplace in an attempt to be elegant.

CARAMEL ICE CREAM

This ice cream has a wonderful burnt-sugar flavor, but what really makes it special is the crushed peanut brittle on top. If you prefer, you may substitute any other kind of nut brittle — macadamia nut is particularly good.

2 cups milk

3 tablespoons flour

2 cups sugar, or more as needed

2 eggs

4 cups heavy cream

Pinch of salt

1 cup peanut brittle, ground until fine

1. Put milk in a double boiler and bring to a boil. Mix flour with ¼ cup sugar and add to milk, stirring constantly with a wooden spoon to avoid lumps. You can also use a food processor to achieve a smooth mixture. Keep warm.

2. Put remaining sugar in a hot, cast-iron frying pan over moderate heat. Let sugar get hot, stirring constantly with a wooden spoon, until it melts and is caramel brown and very smooth.

3. Slowly pour caramel into hot milk, and stir constantly until it is as smooth as glass. (You can also mix in a food processor.) Taste mixture, and if flavor seems too bland, caramelize ¼ cup more sugar — darker this time — and add it.

4. Beat eggs and then blend them into hot mixture, preferably using a food processor. Put aside to cool. You can hold this custard in the refrigerator for 1 day.

5. When ready to freeze, beat cream lightly with salt, and add to cooled mixture.

6. Freeze in an ice-cream freezer according to manufacturer's directions, and serve with peanut brittle topping.

N O T E : This ice cream loses flavor and texture by being frozen more than 24 hours. It is best when served right out of the ice-cream freezer.

Working time: 40 minutes
Preparation time: 1 hour
Serves 8

◆

Opposite: Carrot Roulade (page 85), Caramel Ice Cream, and Warm Pear Tart (page 97)

RICH VANILLA ICE CREAM

This is a basic custard ice cream. Any flavoring in addition to, or instead of, vanilla can be added, such as 2 ounces of melted unsweetened chocolate, strong coffee, pureed fruit, or whatever you wish.

1 cup light cream
1 vanilla bean, cut in half lengthwise
¾ cup sugar
5 egg yolks
2 cups heavy cream, chilled

1. Scald light cream in a heavy pan with vanilla bean and sugar. Remove vanilla bean and scrape seeds back into cream. Discard bean.

2. Beat egg yolks, then slowly add hot cream, making sure not to curdle eggs. Place mixture in a pan over boiling water and beat until mixture is thick and hot, about 5 minutes. Remove from heat, place in a pan set into a bowl of ice water, and continue beating until mixture is room temperature.

3. Add heavy cream, and freeze in an ice-cream freezer according to manufacturer's directions.

N O T E : You can omit vanilla when using another flavor. This mixture does not combine as well with fruit as does Light Vanilla Ice Cream (recipe follows).

Working time: 40 minutes
Preparation time: 1 hour
Serves 6

◆

LIGHT VANILLA ICE CREAM

This basic ice cream is much less rich than the preceding one. Therefore, it is better as a base for fruit purees (See Note).

1 egg
1 cup light cream
¾ cup sugar
1 tablespoon vanilla extract
3 cups heavy cream

1. Put egg, light cream, sugar, and vanilla in a mixer or blender and beat until smooth.

2. Add heavy cream to mixture and beat just until smooth.

3. Freeze in an ice-cream freezer according to manufacturer's directions.

NOTE: If using fruit, puree 2 cups berries and ½ cup sugar in a blender; add this mixture to the cream just before freezing. Two cups of pureed peaches, crushed berries, cooked plums or pears, or other fruit may also be used.

Working time: 10 minutes
Preparation time: 1 hour
Serves 6

◆

MACADAMIA NUT ICE CREAM

Unsalted macadamia nuts are hard to find, but rinsing salted ones works well enough. Sometimes it is possible to buy them glacéed — these don't need further toasting and are the best to use.

10 egg yolks
⅓ cup light brown sugar, packed
2½ cups milk
3 cups heavy cream
¾ cup granulated sugar
½ cup water

1½ cups unsalted macadamia nuts
Butterscotch Sauce (page 163)
Chopped macadamia nuts (optional)

1. Place egg yolks and brown sugar in the bowl of an electric mixer and beat on high until smooth.

2. Scald milk, and heat ½ cup heavy cream.

3. Place granulated sugar and water in a cast-iron frying pan over moderate heat. Cook until sugar melts and turns to a dark caramel syrup, about 5 minutes. Remove from heat and immediately add warm cream, stirring constantly. The mixture will bubble up a good deal.

4. Continue stirring and add hot milk. Mix well, then slowly add caramel mixture to yolks. Pour the mixture back into the saucepan for scalding milk and heat gently until custard coats a spoon. Do not let boil! Remove from heat and chill mixture.

5. Chop nuts. Toast in a 350°F. oven until they are a little darker than they started out, about 5 minutes. Let cool.

6. Whip remaining 2½ cups of cream and fold into caramel custard. Stir in nuts. Freeze in an ice-cream freezer according to manufacturer's directions.

7. Serve with sauce, with additional chopped nuts on top, if desired.

Working time: 25 minutes
Preparation time: 1 hour 15 minutes
Serves 8

◆

ICE-CREAM BOMBE

Bombes are magical creations that take a little practice. They are best made with homemade ice cream or sherbets. They consist of a layer — or two — of ice cream surrounding a bombe mixture, which does not get hard when frozen and is usually made with a cooked syrup beaten into egg yolks. When unmolded, bombes may be covered with meringue and cooked like a Baked Alaska, or they may be decorated with whipped cream (see photograph on page 31).

There are many combinations of ice-cream and bombe flavors that I recommend, including vanilla ice cream and raspberry ice with a chocolate center; caramel ice cream with a chocolate center served with butterscotch sauce; chocolate ice cream with orange bombe mixture; and vanilla ice cream with a layer of crushed praline, then a chocolate mint interior.

2 quarts ice cream, 1 or 2 flavors
Classic or Easy Chocolate Bombe
Mixture (recipes follow)
Ordinary Meringue (page 112) or 1
cup heavy cream, stiffly whipped
Crumb Crust (page 92), unbaked, or
slices of plain sponge cake

1. Freeze a 2- to 3-quart mold or mixing bowl until very cold. Meanwhile, soften 1 flavor of ice cream.

2. Line mold with a smooth layer of ice cream, and refreeze until solid.

3. Line mold with a second layer of ice cream and refreeze if desired.

4. Fill center of mold with bombe mixture and freeze for about 2 hours.

5. Cover top of mold with Crumb Crust mixture or sponge cake layer. Refreeze overnight.

6. Unmold and turn round side up. If using meringue, cover with meringue and bake in a 400°F. oven for 5 minutes. Or cover bombe with whipped cream.

7. Decorate bombe as you wish and serve immediately with an appropriate sauce.

Working time: 1 hour
Preparation time: 24 hours
Serves 10

◆

CLASSIC BOMBE MIXTURE

Aclassic bombe has a texture that is silken smooth and never gets fully hard in the freezer. It should be served within 24 hours. You can use vanilla, mint, chocolate, coffee, orange, or other flavoring.

1 cup water
1½ cups sugar
8 egg yolks

1 cup heavy cream, whipped
12 ounces unsweetened chocolate
(optional)

1. Boil water and sugar to 216°F. or 28° on the saccharometer.

2. Mix 1 cup of syrup with egg yolks, beating constantly. Place bowl over hot water and continue beating until thick and smooth, about 5 minutes.

3. Remove from heat. Place bowl over ice. Beat until cold, adding flavoring as desired. Add whipped cream.

4. Line a 4-quart bombe mold or two 2-quart molds with 1 or 2 thin layers of ice cream and freeze. Then fill inside with bombe mixture, cover with wax paper, and freeze 4 hours or overnight.

5. Unmold and decorate as desired.

Working time: 45 minutes
Preparation time: 5 hours
Serves 8

◆

EASY CHOCOLATE BOMBE MIXTURE

1½ cups heavy cream
3 tablespoons butter
11 ounces semisweet chocolate, cut into small pieces
2 teaspoons vanilla extract or 1 teaspoon mint extract

1. Heat cream with butter in a heavy saucepan.

2. Add chocolate and vanilla or mint extract, and stir until melted.

3. Pour into food processor and process about 1 minute, or until mixture is smooth. Refrigerate until it is thick and very cold.

4. Pour mixture into an ice-cream–lined bombe mold.

N O T E : This mixture is really a chocolate ganache and, after chilling, can be used as a filling for chocolate cake.

Working time: 25 minutes
Preparation time: 3 hours
Makes 2½ cups

◆

RASPBERRY ICE
WITH BING CHERRIES

This ice has always been our family's way of celebrating the fresh Bing cherry season. The problem is that when cherries are at their best, local raspberries are not yet in season. We generally make the ice with frozen raspberries (no sugar added) during the cherry season. Accompanied by a rich chocolate cake, such as a Chocolate Cream Torte (page 64), it makes a memorable combination of textures and flavors.

Blackberries or strawberries may be substituted with some adjustment of lemon juice and sugar. Neither of these berries, however, marries so well with cherries.

1 cup sugar
1 quart fresh or frozen raspberries
½ cup water
Juice of 2 lemons
1 pound Bing cherries, pitted

1. Sprinkle sugar on berries and let stand 2 hours to release juices.

2. Strain raspberries through a fine sieve, such as a *chinois*, or a muslin jelly bag. You should end up with a smooth puree and no seeds.

3. Mix raspberry puree with water and lemon juice. Freeze in ice-cream freezer according to manufacturer's directions.

4. Serve ice in a large bowl, covered with cherries.

NOTE: If using frozen raspberries with syrup or sugar, omit all sugar and add more lemon, if necessary.

Working time: 30 minutes
Preparation time: 3 hours
Serves 6

◆

FRUIT SORBET

Sorbets are a good way to use fruit that is a little too ripe or slightly bruised. At about 120 calories a half-cup, this is a very healthful dessert. (See photograph on page 6.)

2 pounds fresh fruit (See Note)
¼ to ½ cup sugar, or to taste
3 teaspoons lime juice
¼ cup water, or more

1. Peel fruit if appropriate (as for nectarines, pears, or peaches). If using red plums, do not peel.

2. Chop or mash fruit with sugar and lime juice, tasting for tartness.

3. Puree mixture in a food processor and taste again. If too thick, add a little water until mixture is consistency of watery apple sauce.

4. Freeze in an ice-cream freezer according to manufacturer's directions.

N O T E : If using plums, cook for 10 minutes, adding water a tablespoon at a time, to make a thin puree. If using berries, strain out seeds. If mixture loses desired texture by being held in the freezer, you may partly thaw and refreeze in an ice-cream freezer.

Working time: 15–20 minutes
Preparation time: 40 minutes
Serves 6

◆

CHAPTER 3

CAKES, TORTES, ROULADES, AND COOKIES

Checkerboard Cake (page 50)

While tarts are basically one-crust pies, tortes are rich mousselike cakes. They are often low in height and sometimes contain no flour or baking powder. Roulades are cakes, usually of sponge-cake consistency, made in a very thin layer that is rolled up with a whipped cream, jam, or other filling.

Old cookbooks used to say that cakes were one of the first things a young lady was supposed to master, should she desire a suitable spouse. Even today, cakes are immensely useful as part of a buffet, to accompany fruit or ice cream, and, of course, to celebrate a traditional birthday, wedding, or special occasion. But, served on their own, many cakes do not make an elegant dessert for company. It is difficult to serve a guest a good piece of three-layer cake without it falling apart, and when served it is not a particularly pretty shape on the plate. I favor serving traditional cakes in one layer if they are to be used for a formal occasion, or I make many-layer cakes in a loaf shape.

Tortes, on the other hand, are elegant enough for any occasion. They are easy to decorate and to make appear festive or seasonal. Roulades are exceptionally easy to serve in attractive slices, and they attract favorable comment with little work.

Cookies are not really considered desserts on their own, but a few favorites are included here because they complement fruit or ice cream and are invaluable for picnics and buffets. Try baking tiny cookies to serve like petits fours with coffee after dinner, or extra-large cookies to serve as a base for ice cream.

TECHNIQUES

Mixing Cake doughs depend on the action of eggs or baking powder to rise. They should not be beaten to death! I prefer to keep a little flour aside to mix with the baking powder, and I add this mixture at the last moment. Generally I cream the butter and sugar, then add the eggs, beating well. Next I add the flour and liquid a little at a time, alternating the dry with the wet ingredients, and ending with the wet. Many batters are not particular and can be made in a conventional manner. Genoises, however, are fussy; follow the directions exactly. If you feel your cakes could be lighter, try separating the eggs; beat the whites until stiff and fold them in at the last moment.

Baking Most cakes are best baked in pans with removable bottoms. To make the cakes easy to remove, line the pans with a circle of wax paper cut to size. Then coat the pan and paper with nonstick spray and dust with flour, shaking the pan to coat it evenly and tipping it to remove the excess flour. The grease-and-flour combination gives the rising dough something to cling to. If possible, buy insulating bands to put around cake tins. They are excellent for preventing cakes and bar cookies from cooking faster near the outside of the pan than in the center. They are available at kitchenware and baking supply stores.

Most cakes should be cooked at even temperatures of 350°F. or less; you should not open the oven door during the first half of the cooking time, and after that only a crack to take a peek. Cakes are done when a finger pressed on the top does not leave an impression, when the edges look dry and start to pull away from the pan, or when a straw (from a real straw broom, or if you wish to be more sanitary, a cake tester) inserted in the center comes out *almost* dry. There is nothing like experience to help determine the doneness of cakes.

After the cake comes out of the oven, it must be handled with care, for it is now that it is most in danger of collapsing in the center. Keep the cake away from drafts, and allow it to cool slowly and evenly by putting it on a cake rack so the bottom will cool at the same speed as the top. Some cakes, such as savarins and angel food cakes, prefer to be cooled upside down, without the top touching a surface. This is accomplished easily with a tube pan by inverting it over a funnel, but a conventional round cake pan must be supported; prop up the metal edges of the cake pan on other pans, tea cups, or the like. Cakes should be removed from pans when they are lukewarm.

Frosting Frost cakes when they are just warmer than room temperature so the frosting or glaze will spread well. If the cake is very crumbly, it is best to glaze it first, with either melted jam or a thin layer of melted butter, then refrigerate until the surface is hard and dry. After this treatment, frostings will not pick up crumbs and will have a smooth texture. Unless the cake is frosted with whipped cream or buttercream, do not put the cake in the refrigerator or it will become dense, and if it is frosted with chocolate, it will acquire a gray cast. Keep cake leftovers under a loose cover of aluminum foil or a cake cover.

Presentation and Decoration Cakes are most easily handled if you place them on a foil-covered cardboard slightly larger than the diameter of the cake. These cardboards are available at party supply stores, and they make decorating and serving much easier. Roulades are best served on a foil-covered 6 × 24- to 30-inch piece of wood 1 inch thick. Special boards are sold for this purpose, but you can also use a homemade version.

Decorating a cake is the fun part of the process. If you are not an expert, with years of formal cake-decorating background, do not fear. Be original and simple. Master the pastry bag and one or two tips, such as the star tip, so you can make a simple border or a whipped-cream rosette. Stay away from writing on the cake's surface unless you have a steady hand. Use your imagination, and the pictures in magazines and cookbooks, to inspire you. Chocolate leaves, candied fruit, halves of nuts, and crystallized flowers are all simple to make or use. Keep in mind that the cake's decoration should give a clue to its flavor. Glazed apricots, for instance, would not be suitable for a banana-nut cake, but glazed slices of banana or walnut halves would be.

CARAMEL BANANA NUT CAKE

his makes a good family dessert or picnic fare and is also useful for tea parties when cut in small squares. It is a fitting resting place for slightly overripe bananas. Cinnamon, cloves, and nutmeg may be added if a spicier cake is desired. The frosting makes the cake distinctive (see photograph on page 183).

1½ cups sugar
½ cup butter
2 eggs, beaten
1 cup soured milk (See Note) or
    buttermilk
½ cup chopped walnuts or pecans

¼ teaspoon salt
2 teaspoons baking powder
1 teaspoon baking soda
3 to 5 mashed ripe bananas
1 teaspoon vanilla extract
2 cups flour
Caramel Glaze or Frosting
    (pages 185, 186)

1. Preheat oven to 350°F. Grease an 8 × 11-inch pan.

2. Cream sugar and butter until light and fluffy. Add beaten eggs, followed by soured milk, nuts, salt, baking powder, baking soda, bananas, vanilla, and flour. (If bananas are very soft and wet, add up to ½ cup extra flour.)

3. Pour into prepared pan and bake for 35 to 40 minutes or longer, or until a toothpick comes out dry. When lukewarm, cover with Caramel Frosting.

NOTE: To make soured milk, add 1 tablespoon lemon juice to 1 cup milk, and let sit for 1 hour.

Working time: 25 minutes
Preparation time: 2 hours
Serves 10

◆

HUNGARIAN CAKE

This is a rather old-fashioned birthday cake that is very good with ice cream or fruit. It predates by some years the current trend to make every chocolate dessert contain greater and greater concentrations of chocolate. The frosting is very dark and shiny, and is also good on the white cake used to make Coconut Snowballs (page 53).

CAKE

3 eggs, separated
1 cup sugar
1 teaspoon vanilla extract
2 cups sifted cake flour
    (not self-rising)
2 teaspoons baking powder
½ teaspoon salt
1¼ cups heavy cream

HUNGARIAN FROSTING

4 ounces unsweetened chocolate
6 tablespoons butter
2 tablespoons hot water
1 cup confectioners' sugar
2 eggs, lightly beaten

1. Preheat oven to 350°F. Grease two 8-inch round cake pans or one

8 × 12-inch pan.

2. Beat egg yolks with sugar until thick, or until ribbons form when beater is lifted.

3. Add vanilla, then flour, baking powder, and salt, alternating with cream. Beat egg whites, and fold into yolk mixture. Do not mix any more than is necessary to blend.

4. Pour batter into pans and bake for

20 to 30 minutes, or until browned. Remove from pans, then cool slightly.

5. Melt chocolate and butter in a double boiler over hot water. Beat in water and confectioners' sugar, then add eggs. Beat until frosting reaches a spreading consistency. Frost cake while still warm for best appearance.

Working time: 40 minutes
Preparation time: 1½ hours
Serves 10

◆

GENOISE

Genoise is a classic sponge cake and the basis of many desserts. A rather grainy cake, tasting of butter and eggs, it complements frosting well and is best left unflavored. It is particularly good as a base for petits fours. It is tricky and will let you know if you have a heavy hand. If you wish to cheat, you can add 2 teaspoons of baking powder to the flour, which will allow you to be a little less nervous. But serious cooks should learn to make a genoise the authentic way. If the whole idea scares you, make a sponge cake.

4 eggs
½ cup superfine sugar
½ cup butter, clarified
⅞ cup flour

1 teaspoon vanilla extract or other flavoring

1. Preheat oven to 350°F. Butter and flour a 9-inch round cake pan.

2. Beat eggs and sugar in a bowl over hot-to-the-touch water until the mixture is very thick and warm. Remove from hot water and beat until cool.

3. Melt butter over hot water, but do not allow it to get hot.

4. Sift flour and return it to the sifter. Slowly sift the flour over eggs, carefully folding it in with a long-handled, coarse whisk.

5. When all flour is sifted in, begin adding butter and vanilla. You must add butter very carefully. If overmixed, the cake will be heavy and take on a greenish color. Try to sprinkle butter, and do not be afraid to leave some unmixed.

6. Pour batter gently into pan and bake until a cake tester inserted in the center comes out clean, about 30 minutes.

Working time: 20 minutes
Preparation time: 1 hour
Serves 6

◆

FRUIT KUCHEN

This is the very easiest of cakes. The batter can be mixed in a single dish, so clean-up is easy. You can use plums of any type, apples, rhubarb, cranberries, currants, sour cherries, or even underripe pears.

Every German bakery has its own version of this cake, and in most cases it is dry, too sweet, and short on fruit. To make this delicious, you must make a thin cake, and cram as much fruit and streusel as possible on top. And, the tarter the fruit, the better the kuchen will be.

CAKE

½ cup butter
½ cup sugar
Grated peel of 1 lemon
3 eggs
2 cups flour

1 tablespoon baking powder
1 to 2 tablespoons milk
2 pounds fruit (plums, apples, rhubarb, cranberries, currants, sour cherries, or pears)
Cinnamon, nutmeg, and ground cloves

STREUSEL TOPPING

1 cup sugar
1 cup flour
½ cup butter
1½ teaspoons cinnamon

1. Preheat oven to 375°F. Lightly grease two 8-inch cake pans.

2. Put butter, sugar, and lemon peel in a food processor and process until smooth. Add eggs and process 1 minute more. Add flour, baking powder, and milk, and pulse on and off until mixed. Or, mix all by hand in the order given. Do not overmix.

3. Spread batter in pans.

4. If using plums, cut them into quarters or smaller, discarding the pits. Slice apples or pears into neat, thin slices. Slice rhubarb, if using. Arrange fruit of choice decoratively in concentric circles on cakes, pushing one point of each slice or piece of fruit into the dough so the other point sticks up. Sprinkle the fruit with cinnamon, nutmeg, and cloves to taste.

5. Put streusel ingredients in a food processor and pulse until mixed, or mix by hand in a bowl. Work topping into large crumbs with your fingers, then cover cakes with topping. Bake cakes in upper third of oven for 40 to 50 minutes, or until they are lightly browned and pulling away from sides and topping is crisp. Serve lukewarm if possible, with or without heavy cream.

N O T E : I usually make triple batches of streusel and store the excess in the refrigerator (for 2 weeks) or in the freezer (for 6 months).

Working time: 10 minutes
Preparation time: 1 hour
Serves 12 (2 cakes, 6 servings each)

◆

CHECKERBOARD CAKE

Making this cake is a big job, and when you are finished the cake is small, but the recipe can easily be doubled without much additional work. The result is fabulous. A Checkerboard Cake is not only impressive to look at but pleasing to all the sensations (see photograph on page 190). The combinations of tastes, textures, and degrees of sweetness are memorable.

Frosting lovers should note the amount of frosting that is used on this tiny cake. Try making it at least once. It is a good lesson in many of the classic elements of great desserts: genoise, fondant, and buttercream. The fondant should be made at least one week in advance, and it can be stored for several months — therefore I have not included its preparation in the time allowed.

Warning: This cake is addictive. One member of my family attempts yearly to insist that this Checkerboard Cake is the only birthday cake worth having. If you wish to cheat, make a sponge cake and use simpler frostings, but remember that it won't fool the family.

1 12-inch square Genoise (page 48)
2 cups Mousseline Buttercream
    Frosting with chocolate (page 185)
1 cup Apricot Glaze (page 194), warm
1 cup Royal Icing (page 204)
1 cup chocolate-flavored Classic
    Fondant (page 191)
1 cup vanilla-flavored Classic Fondant
    (page 191)
1½ cups toasted sliced almonds

1. Split Genoise into 2 layers with a bread knife, and fill generously with some buttercream. Glaze top and sides of cake generously with Apricot Glaze, repeating on top if necessary to be sure that it is absolutely smooth and that no crumbs are sticking up, making bumps.

2. With ruler and sharp point of knife, draw an uneven number of squares on top of cake. Start squares ½ inch in from edge of cake.

3. Using a paper cone filled with Royal Icing, trace squares, following the knife marks. Let icing set for 25 minutes.

4. Carefully fill in alternate squares with chocolate and vanilla fondant.

5. Spread more buttercream on the sides of cake and pipe a decorative ½-inch border around the top edge.

6. Press toasted almonds thickly into frosting on sides. Refrigerate, if necessary, until ready to serve.

Working time: 1½ hours
Preparation time: 4 hours
Serves 9

◆

COCONUT SNOWBALLS

These large, very heavily iced cupcakes look wonderful at Christmas. They depend on having fresh coconut; if you can't get fresh, don't bother to make them. Packaged sweetened coconut makes the cake entirely too sweet.

Coconut Snowballs will not keep more than 24 hours, because the coconut starts to turn when not very cold, and boiled frosting gets sugary when chilled. They can, however, be made up to 5 hours in advance, if protected from humidity.

For more formal occasions this dessert can be baked in 2 round cake pans, making a very high coconut cake.

⅔ cup butter, at room temperature
1¼ cups sugar
1 teaspoon vanilla extract
3 cups sifted cake flour
    (not self-rising)
3 teaspoons baking powder
½ teaspoon salt
1 cup milk
5 egg whites
¼ teaspoon cream of tartar
1 fresh coconut, cracked open
    and meat peeled and grated
    (See Note)
7-Minute Boiled Icing (page 193)

1. Preheat oven to 325°F. Line 24 muffin cups with paper liners.

2. Cream butter and sugar in a mixer bowl. Add vanilla.

3. Sift flour at least 3 times, then measure, tapping cup slightly so it settles a bit. Keep ½ cup flour in a separate cup, and mix in baking powder and salt.

4. With mixer running, alternately add remaining flour and ¾ cup milk, a little at a time. When smooth, add reserved flour mixture, then remaining ¼ cup milk.

5. Beat egg whites and cream of tartar until stiff peaks are formed, and fold them into batter. Pour into muffin tins. Bake until brown on top and a tester inserted in the center comes out clean, about 12 to 18 minutes. Allow cupcakes to cool thoroughly.

6. Prepare coconut. Crack coconut by taking a heavy screwdriver and placing point near or on one of the "eyes" and hitting it smartly with a hammer. Try to just crack, not to go right into center.

7. After making several cracks, pieces of shell should start to fall off. Break off pieces of shell with your fingers. If ripe, coconut should not stick to the shell. Discard juice, or coconut water.

8. Using a vegetable peeler or sharp knife, peel thin brown skin off the white "meat." Grate coconut meat finely by hand. Handle meat as little as possible.

9. Peel papers off and frost cupcakes completely on all sides except bottom. Immediately cover all icing with as much freshly grated coconut as possible. Allow to dry and harden a bit, but protect snowballs from a humid atmosphere or icing will get sugary. Do not ever put in refrigerator.

NOTE: The coconut should not be opened or grated until you are ready to frost the cake. For noncoconut lovers, melt a little semisweet chocolate and dribble over the frosted Snowballs instead of dipping them in coconut.

Working time: 1 hour
Preparation time: 2½ hours
Serves 15–20

◆

UPSIDE-DOWN CAKE

Upside-down cakes are old-fashioned, delicious, and attractive desserts. If cake is a favorite in your household, try this one-step process, which produces a tasty cake that lasts well and can be served hot, warm, or cool. Upside-down cakes are traditionally made with pineapple, but the same method can be used to produce cranberry, rhubarb, peach, banana, or combination cakes, and many different batters can be used. Here are three topping recipes and the basic cake recipe. Remember that you must make the topping first.

NOTE: With fruits such as cranberries, apples, and rhubarb, melt the brown sugar and water in a saucepan and place in the baking dish, then add the fruit and pour the cake batter on top. Unlike pineapple, they do not need to be browned first.

PINEAPPLE TOPPING

1 cup light brown sugar, packed
3 tablespoons water
4 tablespoons butter
1 fresh pineapple, peeled, cored, and
    sliced into rings

1. Melt brown sugar, water, and butter in a skillet. Add pineapple rings and brown quickly on both sides in this glaze, but do not let them cook.

2. Place rings in a well-greased 10-inch cake pan in a decorative pattern, filling spaces with small pieces of pineapple. Pour brown sugar glaze over, then add batter.

CRANBERRY TOPPING

1 cup light brown sugar, packed
6 tablespoons butter
½ teaspoon cinnamon
12 ounces fresh cranberries

1. Melt brown sugar and butter with cinnamon in a saucepan. Pour into a well-greased 10-inch cake pan and place cranberries on top.

2. Pour batter over fruit and bake.

NOTE: If you prefer, substitute 1 cup marmalade for ¾ cup brown sugar, and add 1 teaspoon freshly grated orange peel.

COCONUT TOPPING

3 tablespoons butter
⅓ cup light brown sugar, packed
1 cup shredded coconut, fresh if
    possible
1 tablespoon flour

1. Spread butter on sides and bottom of a 10-inch cake pan, and sprinkle brown sugar evenly over it. Spread coconut on top of butter and brown sugar, and flour on top of coconut.

2. Pour cake batter on top and bake near bottom of oven.

CAKE BATTER

1 cup sifted cake flour (not self-rising)
1 teaspoon baking powder
4 eggs, separated
1 cup sugar
1 tablespoon butter, melted
1 teaspoon vanilla extract

1. Preheat oven to 350°F. Prepare topping of choice in a 10-inch cast-iron skillet or cake pan.

2. Sift flour with baking powder and set aside.

3. Beat egg yolks with ½ sugar and set aside.

4. Beat egg whites until stiff, and slowly add remaining sugar. Fold

yolks into whites. Add butter and vanilla, then fold in flour.

5. Pour batter on top of topping in skillet and bake for 35 minutes, or until a cake tester inserted in the center comes out clean.

N O T E : To make the cake more interesting, add ground nuts, or replace ½ cup sugar with 1 cup orange marmalade.

Working time: 1 hour
Preparation time: 2 hours
Serves 8

◆

APRICOT CHEESECAKE

Flavored cheesecakes, such as this apricot version, are a nice change from plain ones with fruit toppings.

4 ounces dried apricots
½ cup water
1 tablespoon lemon juice
1⅓ cups sugar
24 ounces cream cheese
6 eggs, separated
Grated zest from 1 lemon
1 teaspoon vanilla extract
1 cup heavy cream
10-inch baked Crumb Crust (page 92),
    in springform pan

1. Preheat oven to 300°F.

2. Cook apricots in a saucepan with water, lemon juice, and ⅓ cup sugar until apricots are soft. Puree in a food processor, then cool.

3. Beat cream cheese in an electric mixer with a beater, not the whisk, until light. Gradually add yolks, lemon zest, vanilla, and cream.

4. Beat whites until stiff, then beat in remaining 1 cup sugar and, when a nice meringue is formed, stir in apricot puree. Fold cream cheese mixture into the apricot–egg white mixture and pour into crust.

5. Bake for about 40 minutes, or until there is no jiggle when cheesecake is moved. Leave in turned-off oven with door slightly ajar for 1 hour,

then chill. Serve colder than room temperature, but not as cold as it is when removed from refrigerator — about 50°F.

NOTE: If desired, the apricot and sugar puree can be omitted and 2 tablespoons finely grated fresh ginger and 1 cup finely chopped candied ginger can be substituted. Make crust with gingersnaps.

Working time: 30 minutes
Preparation time: 4 hours
Serves 12

◆

FRUIT SHORTCAKE

There are 2 kinds of shortcake — one a sponge cake with fruit and the other a baking powder biscuit. This is the latter. There is nothing better than this cake served at teatime with homemade strawberry jam and crème fraîche, or a combination of whipped cream and a little sour cream and sugar. Individual shortcakes can be made by using a cookie cutter and rolling the dough only ½ inch thick.

SHORTCAKE

2 cups plus 2 tablespoons flour
4 teaspoons baking powder
½ teaspoon salt
1 tablespoon sugar
½ cup butter
¾ cup milk
¼ cup heavy cream or melted butter

FRUIT FILLING

6 cups sliced fruit, such as
   strawberries and peaches
Sugar, to taste

Cointreau or other liqueur (optional)
2 cups heavy cream

1. Preheat oven to 400°F. Lightly grease a baking sheet. (Grease with butter for a nice brown bottom.)

2. Stir flour, baking powder, salt, and sugar together. Cut in butter, and add enough milk to form a soft dough, handling as little as possible.

3. With your hands, gently form dough into 2 equal balls. Pat each to a ¾-inch thickness.

4. Place the 2 layers on baking sheet and paint the top of dough with cream or melted butter, and bake for about 12 minutes, or until lightly browned and risen in height.

5. Put about 2 cups of neatest slices of fruit aside for a garnish. Lightly crush remainder of fruit in a bowl with a potato masher, adding sugar to taste and liqueur, if using.

6. Assemble the shortcake by putting one layer a serving plate and covering it with some sliced fruit and a little crushed fruit. Place the second layer on top. Decorate with more of the reserved sliced fruit or whole berries. Surround the shortcake with more crushed fruit, or serve extra crushed fruit in a bowl.

7. Whip cream and place a large rosette of whipped cream in the center. Pass remainder separately, or make generous mounds around base or on top of individual shortcakes.

Working time: 35 minutes
Preparation time: 1 hour
Serves 6

◆

ONE-YEAR-OLD CHRISTMAS FRUITCAKE

This is by far the best fruitcake I have ever tasted. It should be served in very thin slices to special people with tea or hot cider on a cold winter day, in front of the fireplace. You don't have to follow the recipe slavishly; add the total amount of fruit in any proportion that suits you. I usually add more citron and raisins, and often leave out the cherries altogether. All almonds are sometimes preferred to part almonds and part walnuts.

I make triple batches and bake the fruitcakes in a variety of sizes and shapes, so I can eat some now, be sure to have some for next year, and be left with a few small ones to give away. Be sure not to overbake the cakes made in smaller pans!

8 ounces diced candied pineapple

4 ounces halved candied cherries

4 ounces diced candied citron

2 tablespoons diced candied lemon peel

2 tablespoons diced candied orange peel (see page 205)

1⅓ cups light raisins

⅔ cup dark raisins

⅓ cup dried currants

⅔ cup coarsely chopped blanched almonds

1 cup coarsely chopped walnuts

1½ cups flour

¼ teaspoon allspice

¼ teaspoon cinnamon

¼ teaspoon baking soda

3 eggs

¾ cup, or more, good-quality brandy

3 tablespoons applesauce

½ teaspoon almond extract

4 tablespoons butter, softened

½ cup sugar

½ cup light brown sugar, packed

16 blanched almond halves, for garnish

1. Preheat oven to 275°F. Grease a 12-inch ring mold. Line bottom and sides with oiled heavy brown paper or parchment paper and grease again. Or use a well-greased teflon pan. The mixture sticks easily.

2. In a large bowl, combine fruit and chopped nuts. Add ½ cup flour, and mix well.

3. Sift remaining 1 cup flour with allspice, cinnamon, and baking soda.

4. In a medium bowl, beat eggs until light colored. Add ¼ cup brandy, applesauce, and almond extract.

5. In a large bowl, cream butter with sugars. Add egg mixture, then gradually add flour-spice mixture, beating only until combined. Add fruit mixture to batter and mix with your hands or a wooden spoon.

6. Arrange almond halves in pan in a neat pattern, and turn batter into pan and press into all corners, packing down well. Smooth top.

7. Bake for about 2½ hours, or until a cake tester comes out clean. Let the fruitcake cool 30 minutes on a wire rack.

8. Roll a large piece of cotton cheesecloth into a ball. Immerse it in remaining ½ cup brandy. If very wet, squeeze a little brandy back into bowl. Wrap cake in cheesecloth, tucking ends into center hole. Pour any remaining brandy on top, and place cake in a plastic bag and tie tightly.

9. Store cake in a cool cupboard or basement. Although it may be eaten in a week, this fruitcake is best when aged a year. Approximately once a month, remove cheesecloth,

immerse it in more brandy, and re-wrap. When at least half a bottle of brandy has been absorbed, cake is at its best.

NOTE: This fruitcake may be kept for up to two years if given a fresh brandy bath every 3 months after the first 6 months of monthly baths. This is an expensive process that results in a delicious fruitcake.

Working time: 1 hour
Preparation time: 3 hours – 1 year
Serves about 12

◆

CHOCOLATE APRICOT TORTE

This torte can be served accompanied by a bowl of whipped cream mixed with apricot jam slightly thinned with a touch of rum. Bake it one day ahead for best results, or freeze well-wrapped and unglazed.

For the decoration, buy the best dried whole apricots you can find. They should be a nice orange color, not dry and wrinkly.

½ cup minced dried apricots

¼ cup brandy or rum

6 ounces semisweet or bittersweet chocolate, finely chopped

½ cup butter, in small pieces

3 eggs, separated, at room temperature

½ cup plus 3 tablespoons sugar

⅔ cup ground blanched almonds

¼ cup flour

¼ teaspoon cream of tartar

Chocolate Glaze I (page 192)
Glacéed apricots (see Glacéed Fruit, page 202)

1. Preheat oven to 375°F. Grease an 8-inch springform pan with 2-inch-high sides. Line bottom with greased parchment paper or wax paper.

2. Soak apricots in brandy or rum until plumped.

3. Melt chocolate with butter in top of a double boiler over barely simmering water. Stir until smooth. Remove from heat and cool.

4. Beat egg yolks with ½ cup sugar until thick ribbons fall from whisk. Beat in chocolate mixture, then add almonds and flour. Fold in apricots with any remaining liquor.

5. Using clean, dry beaters, beat whites with cream of tartar until soft peaks form. Add remaining 3 tablespoons sugar, 1 tablespoon at a time, and beat until whites are stiff but not dry.

6. Gently fold ⅓ of the whites into batter to lighten it, then fold in remaining whites. Turn batter into prepared pan and bake until a tester inserted in center comes out with moist crumbs, about 35 minutes. Cool cake in pan. Wrap tightly and let stand 1 day at room temperature. (Note: This cake can be prepared up to 3 days ahead, but do not refrigerate.)

7. The next day, remove cake from pan and invert onto a foil-covered cardboard. Spread edges of cake with just enough glaze to smooth away any imperfections. Be careful to keep crumbs out of remaining glaze.

8. Reheat remaining glaze over barely simmering water until smooth and just pourable but not thin and watery, then strain glaze through a fine sieve.

9. Place cake on a bakery turntable or plate. Pour the glaze onto center of cake. Using a dry metal spatula, spread it over top and sides of cake, working glaze as little as possible. Transfer cake to a rack.

10. Arrange glacéed apricots around upper edge. Let glaze set. Serve cake the same day, at room temperature.

Working time: 1 hour
Preparation time: 2 hours
Serves 10

◆

MOCHA WALNUT TORTE

This rich torte can be served in very small pieces. It is a good choice for a buffet, since it serves a large number. The cake is best when kept at about 40°F., but it can be refrigerated if necessary.

Because the cake is flourless, the batter must be handled with care so as not to lose the volume from the beaten eggs. Do not overmix!

½ cup flour or fine bread crumbs, for
    dusting pans
2 pounds shelled walnuts
¼ cup Dutch-process cocoa, sieved
12 eggs, separated
2 cups sugar
⅛ teaspoon cream of tartar
Pinch of salt
Light Buttercream, flavored with
    coffee (page 187)
Glacéed walnut halves (page 202)
Chocolate Curls (page 200)

1. Preheat the oven to 350°F. Grease three 9-inch round cake pans and line the bottoms with greased wax paper. Sprinkle with flour or fine bread crumbs.

2. In a food processor, grind ½ walnuts to a fine powder. Mix with cocoa. Chop other ½ coarsely and set aside for decoration.

3. With an electric mixer, beat yolks and sugar until thick and ribbons form when beater is lifted.

4. In a separate bowl, beat whites with cream of tartar and salt until stiff peaks form.

5. Fold some of whites into yolks, then fold yolk mixture into whites. Add nut-cocoa mixture, folding very carefully so as not to lose too much volume.

6. Divide batter among 3 pans and smooth tops with a spatula. Bake for 45 minutes on middle rack of oven, or until cakes start to pull away from sides of pans and tops feel springy.

7. Remove pans from oven and invert cakes in pans onto racks. Do not remove cakes from pans for 10 to 15 minutes. When slightly warm, run a knife around sides, remove cakes from pans, and set right side up to finish cooling.

8. Spread buttercream thinly on tops of all 3 layers, and stack. Spread sides and top with more buttercream, saving some to pipe through a pastry bag for decoration later.

9. Stick chopped nuts to sides of cake, covering all frosting. Decorate top with rosettes of buttercream, gla-céed walnut halves, and Chocolate Curls.

Working time: 1½ hours
Preparation time: 4 hours, including chilling time
Serves 15–20

◆

CHOCOLATE CREAM TORTE

This is my family's favorite birthday cake. When accompanied by fresh raspberry sherbet topped with pitted Bing cherries, it provides a fitting end to any feast.

CAKE

4 ounces unsweetened chocolate
1 cup milk
5 eggs, separated
2 cups sugar
1 cup pastry flour
1 teaspoon baking powder

FILLING AND FROSTING

5 ounces German's sweet or semisweet chocolate
2¾ tablespoons sugar
3 tablespoons water
3 egg yolks

1½ cups heavy cream plus ½ cup additional for garnish (optional)

1. Preheat oven to 325°F. Generously grease and flour two 9- or 10-inch cake pans.

2. Prepare cake. Melt chocolate in milk in a double boiler, and let it cool.

3. Beat the egg yolks and sugar until thick and ribbons form. Add flour, sifted with baking powder, and chocolate mixture.

4. Beat whites until they make stiff peaks, then fold into chocolate mix-

ture. Pour batter into pans and bake for about 25 minutes, or until tester inserted in center comes out just clean. Cool in pan for 30 minutes. Fill and frost when completely cool.

5. Prepare filling and frosting. Cook chocolate with the sugar and water in a double boiler until it is smooth and thick. Remove from heat and add egg yolks one at a time, stir-ring constantly. Let cool to room temperature.

6. Whip 1½ cups cream until stiff, and fold into chocolate mixture.

7. Spread filling between cake layers, and on top and sides. Decorate with rosettes of stiffly whipped cream, if desired. This cake must be kept re-frigerated, but is best served at about 50°F.

Working time: 40 minutes
Preparation time: 2½ hours
Serves 10–12

◆

SAVARIN WITH FRUIT

Despite the large number of steps, savarins are easy and quite quick to make. This basic recipe has endless variations. Try decorating it with cherries and flavoring it with melted currant jelly and kirsch syrup (Cherry Savarin, page 67). Or use strawberries and Cointreau.

The cake may be frozen after the syrup is applied and before glazing. It will keep frozen for one month. To serve, thaw, cover loosely with foil, and reheat in a 350°F. oven, then glaze and serve immediately. Leftover slices heat nicely in the microwave. They should be served with piping hot sauce and whipped cream.

CAKE

2 tablespoons active dry yeast
Pinch of sugar
⅓ cup lukewarm milk

2 cups flour
3 tablespoons sugar
4 eggs, lightly beaten
6 tablespoons butter, softened

RUM SYRUP

1 cup sugar
2 cups water
½ cup dark rum, preferably Myers's

Apricot Glaze (page 194)
1 to 2 cups canned apricots, peeled if
    possible
¼ cup sliced almonds
Whipped cream
Apricot Rum Sauce (page 181)

1. Prepare cake. Sprinkle yeast and sugar on milk to soften, and stir to dissolve. Let yeast stand for 3 or 4 minutes to proof, or develop gas bubbles on the surface.

2. Sift flour and sugar together into bowl of an electric mixer, and add beaten eggs and yeast mixture. Mix only to blend well. Then, using a dough hook or your hand, knead by slapping against bowl, lifting and stretching dough for about 3 minutes, or until very smooth. The dough will be soft and sticky.

3. Cover dough with plastic wrap. Set it aside to rise in a warm place (75°–85°F.) for about 1½ hours, or until it has doubled in bulk.

4. Punch down dough, and add softened butter. You can knead butter with your fingers, if necessary, to get it smooth and soft. Knead dough with your hands for about 4 minutes, or use a mixer with a dough hook. It will remain soft and sticky.

5. Put dough into a 6-cup savarin mold, 10-inch angel food cake pan, Bundt cake pan, or ring mold. Let it rise in a warm place until it reaches top of mold.

6. Preheat oven to 450°F., then bake savarin for 10 minutes. Lower heat to 350°F., and bake 20 minutes more. The cake is done when top is brown and sides pull away from pan. When you tap cake it should sound hollow. If it browns too quickly, lay a piece of foil loosely over top. Do not overbake or cake will be dry.

7. Allow cake to cool in its pan for 20 minutes. Gently pry cake away from sides and invert onto a cake rack to cool. If necessary, trim bottom so it will stand straight.

8. While cake cools, prepare syrup. Boil sugar with water for 5 minutes. Cool for 5 minutes. Add rum.

9. Set cake on rack over a plate or larger pan to catch drippings, and soak cake repeatedly with rum syrup. Keep applying syrup to sides and top of cake, reusing drippings, until all syrup is used.

10. Paint cake with Apricot Glaze.

11. Decorate with apricots and almonds, then paint apricots with more glaze.

12. Serve savarin warm, accompanied by bowls of whipped cream and Apricot Rum Sauce.

Working time: 1 hour
Preparation time: 4–5 hours
Serves 8

◆

CHERRY SAVARIN

To make a Cherry Savarin, follow the savarin recipe but use Kirsch Syrup, Currant Glaze, and Cherry Sauce (recipes follow). Decorate savarin with cherries dipped in currant jelly and toasted slivered almonds. Fill the center with cherry sauce, or serve the sauce separately.

KIRSCH SYRUP

Substitute kirsch for rum in the recipe for rum syrup.

CURRANT GLAZE

Substitute currant jelly for apricot jam in the glaze recipe.

CHERRY SAUCE

¾ **cup sugar**
2 tablespoons cornstarch

4 cups pitted sour cherries, cooked fresh or canned
8-ounce jar currant jelly (optional)
2 tablespoons lemon juice
3 tablespoons kirsch (optional)

1. Mix sugar and cornstarch and add to cherries. (If there is insufficient juice, add part of a jar of currant jelly.) Add lemon juice.

2. Cook together in a saucepan until mixture is thick and clear, about 4 minutes. Remove from heat and flavor sauce with kirsch if desired.

Working time: 1 hour
Preparation time: 4 hours
Serves 8

◆

GINGER ALMOND COOKIES

Cookies form a wonderful accompaniment to fruit compotes and sorbets and are good for afternoon tea. These Ginger Almond Cookies are very spicy and are wonderful with a glass of cold, unpasteurized cider (see photograph on pages 68–69).

1½ cups butter
1½ cups sugar
¾ cup molasses, preferably dark unsulphured
4 cups flour
1½ teaspoons baking soda
1 tablespoon powdered ginger
1 tablespoon ground cloves
1½ cups roughly chopped almonds

1. Cream shortening, sugar, and molasses until fluffy, by hand or with an electric mixer.

2. Sift flour, then measure and sift again with baking soda, ginger, and cloves. Stir into molasses mixture. Add almonds and mix just until blended.

3. Shape dough into 2 cylinders, each about 2 inches in diameter. Wrap in wax paper and refrigerate several hours, or until very firm. (The dough may be frozen at this stage.)

4. Preheat oven to 350°F.

5. Cut dough into ¼-inch slices. Place slices on a lightly greased baking sheet. Bake for 12 to 15 minutes. Do not allow to color to a dark brown or they will lose flavor. Ideally they should be very crunchy, yet just a tiny bit chewy. Cool on a wire rack.

N O T E : Molasses varies in taste and quality. Take the trouble to find a really good dark unsulphured molasses. Avoid the standard grocery store varieties. If you are unable to find good molasses, substitute brown sugar for granulated. The cookies will have a stronger taste.

Working time: 1 hour
Preparation time: 3–4 hours
Makes about 7 dozen cookies

◆

Previous page: Tea with Hermits (page 79), Apricot Rounds (page 73), Caramel Chocolate Cookies (page 72), and Ginger Almond Cookies (page 70)

SARAH BERNHARDTS

I fell in love with these special cookies at a bakery near my home. When the bakery went out of business, I had to learn how to make them. Macaroons are wonderful cookies to have by themselves after a rich dinner or with sorbet, or served with after-dinner coffee made in little mounds about 1 inch across, and baked for just a few minutes. A chocolate chip or piece of candied violet stuck in the top makes them festive. Miniature versions of Sarah Bernhardts will be well received on a plate of petits fours served with coffee.

MACAROONS

1⅓ cups blanched almonds
1½ cups sifted confectioners' sugar
5 egg whites
½ teaspoon almond extract (optional)

GANACHE

4 cups heavy cream
1 pound semisweet chocolate
1 tablespoon rum, crème de cacao,
    brandy, or Amaretto (optional)

Chocolate Glaze I (page 192)
Chopped almonds (optional)

1. Preheat oven to 300°F. Line a baking sheet with parchment or heavy-duty foil. If using foil, spray with nonstick coating.

2. Put almonds and confectioners' sugar in a food processor and process until mixture is very fine. Add egg whites and almond extract, if desired, and process again until well mixed. The resulting paste should be very thick and hold its shape. If too soft, add a little more confectioners' sugar to stiffen it.

3. Place mixture in a pastry bag with a plain round tip. Pipe mounds about 2 inches in diameter and ⅜ inches high on baking sheet. Keep some space in between, as they will spread. Bake until they start to color, about 20 minutes. Do not overbake, since they will not be good if they are dried out. Remove from baking sheet at once and cool. Store in an airtight box for a few days, if necessary.

4. Cook cream and chocolate in a saucepan over low heat. When chocolate has melted, turn into a food processor and process for 30 seconds, until thick and smooth.

5. If flavoring is desired, add rum, crème de cacao, brandy, or Amaretto to taste. Beat until mixture is lighter in color and texture. Cover with plastic wrap and refrigerate at least 3 hours.

6. To assemble, use either a pastry bag with a large plain tip or a spoon to put a 2-inch-high dollop of ganache on each macaroon. (If using a spoon, smooth the surface with a wet knife.) Refrigerate until ganache is very cold again.

7. Dip each cookie in lukewarm Chocolate Glaze I, and decorate with a few chopped nuts if desired. Refrigerate until ready to serve.

NOTE: You can save one early step by buying a good-quality marzipan and mixing that with egg whites. Or you can buy almond paste, which is simply ground almonds, and add sugar and whites.

Chocolate macaroons are made by adding 3 ounces semisweet chocolate, melted and cooled, and 2 tablespoons cocoa to the mixture before baking.

Working time: 1 hour
Preparation time: 5 hours
Makes 20

◆

CARAMEL CHOCOLATE COOKIES

These very rich cookies are a favorite with children and chocoholics. They are suitable for tea, picnics, and brown-bag lunches, and they freeze well.

2 cups flour
1¾ cups light brown sugar, packed
1½ cups butter, softened

1 cup chopped pecans
2 cups semisweet chocolate chips, or more as desired

1. Preheat oven to 350°F. Lightly grease a 12 × 8-inch pan.

2. In a bowl, combine flour and 1 cup brown sugar. With a fork, stir in ½ cup butter until mixture resembles coarse crumbs.

3. Press mixture into bottom of pan. Sprinkle with pecans. Set aside.

4. In a saucepan, combine remaining 1 cup butter and ¾ cup brown sugar and cook over medium heat, stirring constantly, until the mixture boils. Continue stirring and boil 1 minute, or until mixture blends. Pour over prepared base in pan and bake for 15 to 20 minutes, or until surface is bubbly.

5. Remove from oven and immediately sprinkle chocolate chips evenly over surface. (You can use up to 4 cups of chocolate chips to get a thicker layer of chocolate.) Let stand 1 minute to melt, then spread chocolate with a fork.

6. Cool completely until chocolate is set, then cut into 2-inch squares.

Working time: 15 minutes
Preparation time: 45 minutes
Makes 24 squares

◆

APRICOT ROUNDS

Although these are a challenge to make, they are the favorite cookies of all who taste them at my house (see photograph on pages 68–69). The dough is difficult to handle unless it is frozen. Though not quite as good as fresh baked, the extras may be stored in the freezer well wrapped.

½ cup sugar
3 cups flour
1½ cups butter (about ½ sweet butter), in small pieces
1 teaspoon vanilla extract

1 tablespoon fresh lemon juice
8-ounce jar apricot jam
½ cup sliced blanched almonds, roasted and coarsely chopped
¼ cup confectioners' sugar

1. Sift sugar with flour. Add butter and cut in with a knife and fork, or use a pastry blender, until bits are smaller than barley.

2. Add vanilla and work ingredients into a smooth dough. Wrap in plastic and chill thoroughly.

3. Cut dough in at least 3 equal pieces. Roll out each piece ⅛ inch thick between 2 sheets of floured wax paper, lifting top sheet from time to time so it won't stick. With bottom paper still attached, transfer to a baking sheet and freeze.

4. Preheat oven to 325°F.

5. Remove 1 sheet of rolled pastry at a time from freezer, and turn upside down on a second sheet of floured wax paper. Peel off top sheet and cut out 2-inch rounds with a cookie or biscuit cutter. Transfer rounds to an ungreased baking sheet.

6. Using a smaller cookie cutter, cut out centers from half of rounds, making doughnut-shaped rings to use for tops. The dough scraps can be rerolled and frozen for more cookies. Bake rings and rounds for 15 minutes, or until just barely colored. Let cool on a rack.

7. Add lemon juice to apricot jam and heat until melted. Rub mixture through a coarse strainer, then let cool slightly.

8. Spread rounds with warm strained apricot jam. Lay rings on rounds and sprinkle exposed jam with chopped blanched and roasted almonds, then sift a tiny amount of confectioners' sugar over each cookie.

N O T E : These cookies freeze well if you omit the confectioners' sugar until just before serving.

Working time: 2 hours
Preparation time: 3 hours
Makes about 48

◆

BUTTERSCOTCH BROWNIES

These are the easiest of all cookies, and they keep well in a tightly covered tin. They require only one pan and a wooden spoon for mixing, and the ingredients are usually on hand.

Butterscotch Brownies are rich and chewy. To make a more conventional version, use 2 cups of flour and bake 5 minutes less. It is best to put insulation tape (available at baking supply stores) around the edge of your pan, because the edges tend to dry before the center is cooked.

10 tablespoons butter
2½ cups light brown sugar, packed
2 eggs
1¾ cups flour
2 teaspoons baking powder
1 teaspoon vanilla extract
1 cup coarsely chopped pecans,
    hazelnuts, or walnuts (optional)
1 cup chocolate chips (optional)

1. Heat oven to 325°F. Lightly grease an 8 × 12-inch pan with 2-inch sides.

2. Melt butter in a saucepan over low heat. Remove from heat and stir in brown sugar. Allow to cool, then stir in eggs.

3. Mix flour and baking powder, and add to sugar mixture, followed by vanilla extract, nuts, and chocolate chips.

4. Spread batter smoothly in pan. Bake for about 35 minutes, or until brownies are dry-looking on surface and edges are just pulling away from pan. Do not overbake, or brownies will be dry and hard; if slightly undercooked, they will stay chewy. Cut into bars while warm.

NOTE: For variety, add ½ cup coconut or ½ cup finely chopped dates instead of the nuts and chocolate chips.

Working time: 10 minutes
Preparation time: 55 minutes
Makes 24–30 brownies

◆

BROWNIES

This recipe is nice because it can be made in one pot by hand very easily, so it is well suited for the primitive circumstances of boats, campers, or the woods. You can even cook these brownies in a Dutch oven. The art to making brownies is to be sure they are not baked too long. Always err on the side of undercooking.

2 ounces unsweetened chocolate
½ cup butter
1 cup sugar
2 eggs
½ teaspoon vanilla extract
¼ cup flour
1 cup chopped walnuts (optional)

1. Preheat oven to 325°F. Grease an 8-inch square pan.

2. Combine chocolate and butter in a saucepan and melt over low heat.

3. Stir in sugar, then beat in eggs and vanilla.

4. Stir in flour and walnuts, if using.

5. Spread batter in pan and bake for 40 to 50 minutes, or until springy but still moist. Cut into squares while warm.

NOTE: I usually double this recipe and freeze half.

Working time: 10 minutes
Preparation time: 50 minutes
Makes 16 or more brownies

◆

HERMITS

Hermits are included in this book primarily because they are wonderful as picnic fare or as an accompaniment to fresh fruit. They freeze well, and keep for several days in a covered tin if they are not overbaked. They should be a little chewy in the middle (see photograph on pages 68–69). The traditional hermit is flavored with coffee, which can be substituted for the orange juice and peel in this recipe. Another variation is to substitute 2 cups of well-drained mincemeat plus 1 tablespoon of brandy for the dark or light raisins.

½ cup butter
½ cup vegetable shortening
2 cups light brown sugar, packed
2 eggs
½ cup fresh orange juice
1 tablespoon grated orange peel
3½ cups flour
1 teaspoon baking soda
1 teaspoon freshly ground nutmeg
1 teaspoon cinnamon
2½ cups raisins, dark or light
1¼ cups chopped walnuts or pecans

1. Cream butter, shortening, and brown sugar, then add eggs and mix thoroughly. Stir in orange juice and grated orange peel.

2. Sift flour with baking soda, nutmeg, and cinnamon, and add to creamed mixture.

3. Add raisins and nuts, then chill dough for at least 1 hour.

4. Preheat oven to 400°F. Lightly grease a cookie sheet. Drop rounded spoonfuls of dough about 2 inches apart on baking sheet, then bake 8 to 10 minutes, or until only a slight impression remains when you press a finger on the center.

Working time: 15 minutes
Preparation time: 2 hours
Makes about 7 dozen cookies

◆

SHORTBREAD WITH NUT TOPPING

Shortbread is easy to make and is delicious on its own, but it is transformed into an elegant treat when crowned with this optional nut topping.

SHORTBREAD

1¼ cups flour
3 tablespoons sifted confectioners'
    sugar
10 tablespoons cold butter, in
    small pieces
1 teaspoon vanilla extract
3 tablespoons ice water, more or less

OPTIONAL NUT TOPPING

5 tablespoons butter
½ cup light brown or granulated sugar
3 tablespoons heavy cream
1 tablespoon flour
1 cup sliced blanched almonds or
    pecan halves

1. Put flour and confectioners' sugar in a food processor with butter. Process until consistency of fine meal.

2. With processor on, add vanilla and water, then turn off almost at once.

3. Turn out dough onto a board and, handling as little as possible, bring it together and press it into two 8-inch round cake pans or 8-inch square forms. Cover and refrigerate for at least 1 hour.

4. Preheat oven to 400°F. Score dough ⅛ inch deep in pie-shaped wedges if round, and in 2-inch squares if square. Prick dough all over with a fork so it will not bubble. Bake for 15 minutes, or until lightly brown.

5. If desired, cut while still warm and serve as soon as possible, or cover with nut topping.

6. To prepare topping, melt butter and sugar in a saucepan, and stir in cream and flour, taking care not to form lumps. Bring to a boil, then remove from heat and add nuts.

7. Spread topping on shortbread and bake at 400°F. until top is bubbly and brown, about 15 minutes more.

Working time: 25 minutes
Preparation time: 30 minutes
Makes 32 squares

◆

GINGERBREAD AND APPLE COBBLER

Cobblers consist of a batter baked over fruit. They are rather simple, old-fashioned desserts — not fussy to make and very satisfying to serve. They can be served hot or cold, and are patient about waiting for slow guests.

APPLE TOPPING MIXTURE

½ cup dark brown sugar, packed
4 tablespoons butter
¼ cup dark unsulphured molasses
3 tablespoons water
3 medium baking apples

CAKE

1⅓ cups flour
1 teaspoon baking powder
¼ teaspoon baking soda
½ teaspoon cinnamon
2 teaspoons ground ginger
¼ teaspoon allspice
½ teaspoon ground cloves
6 tablespoons butter
¾ cup dark brown sugar, packed
⅔ cup dark unsulphured molasses
⅔ cup milk
½ teaspoon vanilla extract
1 cup heavy cream
Sugar (optional)

1. Preheat oven to 300°F.

2. Combine brown sugar, butter, mo-lasses, and water in a saucepan over medium heat, stirring until smooth. Pour into a 10-inch soufflé dish, or a casserole of equal volume with fairly steep sides.

3. Peel and slice apples and place on top. Cover loosely with foil and bake for 15 minutes, or until lightly cooked. Turn oven to 350°F.

4. While apples are baking, sift together flour, baking powder, baking soda, cinnamon, ginger, allspice, and ground cloves.

5. Melt butter, brown sugar, and molasses in a saucepan. Add milk and vanilla. (Note: At this point the mixtures can all be set aside. It takes only a minute to combine and get them into the oven.)

6. Stir flour mixture into molasses mixture, beating just until incorporated and no lumps of flour show. Pour into baking dish on top of apples and bake for 25 to 30 minutes, or until top is light and springy.

7. Whip cream, adding sugar if desired. Serve at once with whipped cream passed separately.

N O T E : This is an interesting variation on gingerbread. Quick and easy, the cake can be made without the apples, but the quantities should be doubled. The butter, brown sugar, and molasses from the topping will become a caramel sauce on the bottom of the gingerbread.

Working time: 30 minutes
Preparation time: 1 hour
Serves 6

◆

BRANDY SNAPS

These lovely, spicy, old-fashioned cookies, which go well with fruit and ice cream, are easy to make after just a little practice and with no distractions. The trick is to remove the warm cookies at the moment when they start to harden and then quickly roll them on a finger, wooden spoon, or broom handle. They may also be rolled into a cone shape to be filled later with Crème Chantilly (page 175; see photograph on page 127). Store Brandy Snaps in a dry, well-sealed cookie tin.

The quality of molasses used is of extreme importance. It should be dark, thick, unsulphured, and have a good flavor.

½ cup molasses
½ cup butter, in pieces
⅞ cup flour
⅔ cup sugar
1 tablespoon ground ginger
1 tablespoon brandy

1. Preheat oven to 275°F. Line a cookie sheet with heavy-duty foil and grease generously with oil or butter.

2. Heat molasses to boiling point. Add butter slowly, stirring constantly.

3. Sift flour with sugar and ginger, then add to molasses. Add brandy.

4. Drop small portions of batter from

the tip of a spoon onto cookie sheet, leaving space for cookies to spread. Bake for about 16 minutes, or until dark but not burned. Allow to cool slightly, then remove with a wet knife and roll while hot.

Working time: 45 minutes
Preparation time: 1 hour
Makes 40 snaps

◆

Opposite: Ginger Roll (page 84) and Dione Lucas Chocolate Roulade

DIONE LUCAS CHOCOLATE ROULADE

During World War II, while chocolate and sugar were rationed, this dessert was the main attraction of the Cordon Bleu, a restaurant in New York founded by my mother and Dione Lucas, the world's first television cook.

Chocolates vary a great deal in the percentage of fat they contain. I prefer one low in fat for this recipe, such as Maillard Eagle Sweet.

If you don't have a long narrow tray on which to serve this dessert, cover a 6 × 24-inch piece of wood 1 inch thick with aluminum foil, or use several thicknesses of cardboard cut that size and taped together.

10 ounces sweet chocolate

2 tablespoons water

8 eggs, separated

2 cups sugar

1½ cups heavy cream, whipped

3 tablespoons cocoa powder

1. Preheat oven to 350°F. Line a 10 × 15-inch jelly-roll pan with wax paper and oil paper.

2. Melt chocolate and water in a saucepan over low heat. Cool to room temperature.

3. Cream egg yolks with sugar.

4. Beat egg whites until peaks are quite stiff.

5. Add chocolate to yolk mixture, then fold in whites. Pour batter into pan and bake in middle of oven until set, about 20 minutes. Cover with a

damp towel and set in refrigerator overnight, or until chilled.

6. Place cake upside-down on a table, so that towel is on bottom, and remove pan and paper. Spread chocolate sheet with whipped cream and sprinkle with cocoa.

7. Grasping towel and stretching it tightly between your hands, roll up roulade lengthwise like a jelly roll and place on a board or long tray, seam side down. The top will un-doubtedly be cracked and can be pushed together gently with your hands. Decorate the roulade with additional whipped cream or cocoa-sugar mix if desired. Chill in refrigerator before serving.

N O T E : This flourless cake is delicate to handle — it must not be overcooked or it will be too dry to roll. It will invariably crack on the top when rolled, but this does not diminish the looks or the flavor.

Working time: 25 minutes
Preparation time: 3 hours
Serves 8–10

◆

GINGER ROLL

This rather unusual jelly roll is very popular, since the flavor of ginger is somewhat uncommon in desserts (see photograph on page 83). The quality of ginger marmalade used is of great importance. If Keiller's is unavailable, use a brand that is not too sweet. If it is sweet, add some finely cut up crystallized ginger and a touch of lemon juice.

4 eggs
1 cup granulated sugar
2 tablespoons frozen orange juice concentrate, thawed
1 tablespoon grated orange rind
1 cup flour

1 teaspoon baking powder
1 teaspoon powdered ginger
½ teaspoon cinnamon
1½ cups ginger marmalade, preferably Keiller's
1 cup heavy cream
2 tablespoons superfine sugar

1. Preheat oven to 375°F.

2. Beat eggs with an electric beater for at least 5 minutes. Gradually add sugar and continue beating until very thick and smooth, another 3 to 5 minutes.

3. Fold in orange juice and rind.

4. Combine flour, baking powder, ginger, and cinnamon, and sift together over beaten eggs, folding mixture in with a rubber spatula.

5. Pour batter into two 10 × 15-inch jelly-roll pans or one 12 × 24-inch pan, lined with oiled wax paper. Bake for 15 to 17 minutes, or until cake starts to pull away at edges and feels firm to finger.

6. Turn cakes out onto 2 long, overlapping pieces of wax paper. Peel off top paper gently. Roll up cake and bottom paper along long axis and allow to cool. You can put it in refrigerator overnight if necessary.

7. Warm marmalade in a saucepan over low heat with a few tablespoons of water, then allow it to cool to just above room temperature. Whip cream until stiff, adding superfine sugar.

8. Unroll cake and spread with a light coating of marmalade. Cool to room temperature, then spread with whipped cream. Reroll cake without bottom paper and place on a serving board, seam side down. Spread remaining marmalade over top and sides of cake.

Working time: 30 minutes
Preparation time: 2 hours
Serves 12

◆

CARROT ROULADE

On the dessert table, carrots are normally seen only in carrot cake. This Carrot Roulade is a nice change and can easily be improvised on (see photograph on page 35). As an alternative, try frosting the roulade with ginger marmalade, or using orange peel and frozen orange juice concentrate instead of lemon peel and lemon juice in the icing. Whipped cream makes an easy filling. As an alternative filling, you could use orange marmalade mixed with whipped cream.

CAKE

6 eggs, separated
1 cup sugar
¼ cup kirsch
1 cup grated carrots
1½ cups ground almonds
½ teaspoon cinnamon
½ teaspoon mace
1 teaspoon powdered ginger
1 tablespoon baking powder

FILLING

1 pound cream cheese, at room
   temperature
1 cup butter, at room temperature
¼ cup sugar
2 tablespoons grated orange peel
1 tablespoon grated lemon peel
1 teaspoon lemon juice
½ cup chopped pecans (optional)

Double recipe Royal Icing (page 204)
Confectioners' sugar, for garnish

1. Preheat oven to 375°F.
2. Beat egg yolks and sugar in an electric mixer until they are light in color and thick ribbons form when beater is lifted.
3. Gently fold kirsch, carrots, and almonds into yolks by hand. Mix cinnamon, mace, ginger, and baking powder, and sift over top.
4. Beat whites until stiff, and fold into carrot mixture.
5. Line a 10 × 15-inch jelly-roll pan with oiled wax paper, and pour batter in. Bake for 15 to 18 minutes, or until puffy and tan on top and firm to touch.
6. Invert cake onto a smooth dish towel that has been dusted with confectioners' sugar. Gently remove wax paper and replace with a fresh piece. Roll along long axis and cover with towel until cool.
7. Beat all ingredients for filling together, and spread over cake. Roll into a log with seam side down.
8. Paint Royal Icing on roulade with a feather pastry brush. Then refrigerate until ready to serve. The roulade may be made ahead and frozen before being iced, in which case you should defrost, ice, and then serve.

Working time: 30 minutes
Preparation time: 2 hours
Serves 8–12

◆

CHAPTER 4

TARTS AND PIES

Sand Tarts (page 100)

What could be prettier than a fluted tart filled with glazed strawberries? Tarts, which are one-crust pies, are easy, quick, and impressive desserts. Often they are made with a base of short crust pastry, which is structurally sounder than normal pie pastry and enables them to be served without the tin in which they were baked. Tarts are normally served at room temperature and filled with a less juicy mixture than pies, which have a more delicate, flaky crust and often need the support of the pie pan, at least until cut in slices. Pies are usually double-crusted and baked with a flaky butter crust.

The most useful crusts for tarts are short crust pastry, crumb crusts, puff pastry, and meringue bases. Recipes for these and other crusts are included in this chapter.

Short crust pastry is the most versatile and strongest of the tart pastries. It is also the standard pastry for quiches of all kinds. Flaky pie pastry is the normal pastry for pies. It makes nice individual tarts, and is also useful for all kinds of savory fillings. Crumb crusts are wonderful for cheesecakes, and make a good base for any creamy filling such as lemon meringue, Bavarian cream, ice-cream mixtures, or fruit mixed with whipped cream. Cream cheese pastry is less delicate to handle than flaky pastry and is well suited for small turnovers and tarts that require more handling than is desirable for flaky pastry. Puff pastry is used for rectangular fruit flans, and can be made in layers separated by cream or custard mixtures to make napoleons. The pastry scraps make nice cookies when sprinkled with sugar and baked. Unlike other tart and pie pastries, puff pastry rises into a many-layered, flaky structure.

TART PANS

Tarts are best baked in fluted, vertical-sided pans or springform pans that have removable bottoms. Removable bottoms help ensure that the tart will not break apart when it is separated from the pan for presentation. Tart pans come in a variety of sizes and shapes (oblong, square, round) that enable you to vary your presentation: 9-, 10-, and 12-inch sizes, serving approximately 6, 8, and 10 people, respectively, are the most useful. Apple Tart Tatin and other juicy tarts require a 1-piece pan with higher sides, since they collect juices in the bottom.

HANDLING TART AND PIE PASTRY

When preparing short crust pastry or pie pastry, it is essential to handle the dough as little as possible. The easiest method is to put the flour in a food processor, add the very cold shortening cut into small pieces, and then process just until the mixture resembles fine meal. From this point on, mix and handle the dough as little as possible. With the processor off, add the egg (for short crust pastry), then process a few seconds. Next, turn the processor on and add the water, processing just long enough to make the dough start to clump together. Be careful not to let the processor run too long.

Turn out the dough onto a floured board and bring it together, pressing gently into a round, with your fingers. Wrap in wax paper and chill for at least 30 minutes to firm up. (The dough may be left refrigerated for up to 24 hours.) Roll it out between floured sheets of wax paper to about 3 inches larger than the size of the tart pan and ¼ inch thick. Peel off the top paper and pick up the dough by reaching under the lower paper with your hand. Flip the dough onto the tart pan upside-down and peel off the remaining paper. Gently conform the dough to the pan, pressing it into the fluted sides. Trim any dough that reaches over the top of the pan with a knife or by pressing the top with a rolling pin to leave a neat finish. Prick the tart bottom all over with a fork, then chill it in the refrigerator or freeze for later use.

BAKING TARTS

Start with a hot oven (400° or 450°F.) so that the pastry will bake fast. If baked slowly, the butter in the pastry will melt and leave a tough crust. After 7 to 10 minutes, the oven should be reduced to moderate (350°F.) so that the crust will cook through without burning.

"Blind" crusts are cooked before they are filled. For these, line the pan with pastry, prick the bottom with a fork so it will not bubble, and lay a piece of foil on the bottom. Then put in pie weights to hold the bottom flat. Traditionally, uncooked rice or dried beans were used, but now little globs of metal, which can be used over and over, are sold for that purpose. On occasion, I have even used small pebbles, such as found in pea stone driveways. Bake the tart for about 10 minutes, then remove the foil and weights and continue baking until the pastry is dry and golden in color.

Freezing Tart dough freezes well, either baked or unbaked. I usually make 3 or 4 shells at a time and freeze the unused ones unbaked. They keep frozen for several months if well wrapped, but are always better if used within several days.

Fillings A stiff pastry cream is the classic filling for fruit flans. I prefer the cream cheese filling (page 193) or a simple glaze of jam or jelly. If the tart is not assembled until the last moment, the fruit will not moisten the pastry and make it soggy. If it must be done in advance, then a filling should be used to keep the fruit juices from penetrating the crust.

FLAKY PIE PASTRY

This is a traditional pie pastry but it is also nice for individual tarts and for covering deep-dish pies. Shortening, such as Crisco, will produce a lighter, flakier pastry than butter, but the flavor is better with butter.

1½ cups flour
⅔ cup butter, in small pieces
Ice water, as needed

1. Put flour in a large bowl and cut in butter, using a knife and fork or a pastry blender, until largest lump is the size of a grain of rice.

2. Add as little water as possible and mix with your hands just until incorporated. Form dough into a ball, wrap, and refrigerate at least 30 minutes or overnight.

3. Roll out dough to about a ⅛-inch thickness, depending on use, and use to line a pie plate or individual tart shells. For prebaking instructions, see chapter introduction.

Working time: 10 minutes
Preparation time: 1 hour
Makes enough pastry for one 10-inch shell

♦

SHORT CRUST PASTRY

Although the easiest method of making short crust pastry is in a food processor (see page 89), here is the classic method of making it by hand.

1 pound flour
2 teaspoons sugar
1 egg
10 ounces butter, chilled
½ cup ice water

1. Weigh flour and butter, since proportion of butter to flour is important. Shape flour into a mound in middle on a marble slab or other smooth cool surface and make a well in center. Put sugar and egg into well.

2. Knead butter and place it in center of flour well. Begin kneading mixture with about 4 ounces water. When all flour has been mixed in, press dough out twice with palm of your hand.

3. Roll dough into a ball and wrap in a damp cloth. Chill until ready to use. (This dough is better if made the day before and refrigerated.)

4. When ready to use, roll out dough to about a ¼-inch thickness on a lightly floured board. Use for all kinds of flans and tarts. To prebake, see chapter introduction.

NOTE: Omit the sugar in this pastry when using for quiches and other savory tarts.

Working time: 25 minutes
Preparation time: 2 hours
Makes enough pastry for two 10-inch shells

◆

CRUMB CRUST

1½ cups graham cracker crumbs
6 tablespoons butter, melted
¼ cup sugar

1. Preheat oven to 350°F. Butter a 10-inch springform pan or 9-inch pie plate, depending on recipe.

2. Mix graham cracker crumbs, butter, and sugar in a bowl. Press into baking dish, then use a slightly smaller, similar pan to press crumbs into place and make smooth.

3. Chill crust for at least 10 minutes, then bake for 10 minutes. Cool before filling.

NOTE: Any dry cookies can be used to make this crust. Chocolate wafers, some of the Pepperidge Farm cookies, and vanilla- or orange-flavored cookies all make good crusts.

Working time: 10 minutes
Preparation time: 45 minutes
Makes one crust

◆

EASY PUFF PASTRY

This pastry can be used as a basis for fruit tarts, to make napoleons, or for wrapping pears to be baked. You can substitute instant granular flour (such as Wondra Instant Flour) for both flours.

1 cup flour
1 cup sifted pastry flour
½ cup ice water
1 cup chilled butter, in small pieces

1. Remove 1 tablespoon of each kind of flour and set aside. Combine flours and mix well. Either by hand or using an electric mixer, stir flours and water until just combined.

2. Add butter and mix until distributed evenly. Gather dough into a ball and chill for 5 minutes.

3. Using the 2 tablespoons of reserved flour, dust a pastry board. Roll out dough to an 8 × 12-inch rectangle.

4. Fold short ends of dough to meet in the center, then fold in half at center. This is a turn.

5. Turn dough 180°, and repeat steps to make a second turn. Repeat for a third turn.

6. Cover loosely with moisture-proof paper and refrigerate overnight, or up to 3 days. You can freeze dough for 1 month if well wrapped.

7. When ready to use, remove and let warm only slightly. Then roll out dough on a chilled board until it is about ¼ inch thick, and cut to size needed for your use.

8. As with classic puff pastry, this should be baked in a 400°F. oven.

Working time: 30 minutes
Preparation time: 24 hours
Makes enough pastry for one 8 × 12-inch shell

◆

CREAM CHEESE PASTRY

This versatile dough is excellent for making all kinds of turnovers. It tends to be a little less permeable to fruit juices and retains its texture well. The dough can be stored in the refrigerator uncooked for several days, or in the freezer for several weeks.

1 cup butter
8 ounces cream cheese
2 cups flour
1 to 2 tablespoons ice water (optional)

1. Place butter and cream cheese in a food processor and process until absolutely smooth. Add flour and pulse until mixture just comes together. A tablespoon or two of ice water may be added if necessary to bring dough together.

2. Turn out dough onto wax paper

and mold into a ball. Wrap it well and refrigerate for at least several hours — overnight is best.

3. Preheat oven to 350°F. Roll dough out between sheets of floured wax paper to an ⅛-inch thickness, or whatever thickness your recipe requires. Handle as little as possible. For a prebaked pie shell, transfer to a pie pan, place foil on top, and fill with pie weights. Bake for 1 to 5 minutes. Remove pie weights and foil, and bake until crust is tan, another 5 to 10 minutes.

N O T E : This pastry can be made with low-fat cream cheese to reduce the calories with only a little flavor and texture loss. To make turnovers, cut pastry into squares, put filling on each, then fold and seal with an egg wash made with 1 egg beaten with 2 tablespoons water.

Working time: 10 minutes
Preparation time: 1 hour
Makes enough pastry for one 10-inch shell

◆

RASPBERRY·RHUBARB PIE

This is a quick and attractive dessert, if you keep pie or tart shells in the freezer, for those times when rhubarb is available in the market or in your garden. Don't ever wash raspberries! They wilt, lose their shape, and taste terrible.

Zest of 1 orange (only zest, not white pith)
⅓ cup sugar
2 tablespoons cornstarch
10-inch Flaky or Short Crust Pastry (pages 90, 91) shell, glazed with beaten egg white and prebaked

1 pound fresh rhubarb, cut into 1-inch diagonal pieces
2 cups fresh raspberries
1 8-ounce jar seedless raspberry jam
2 tablespoons water
1 tablespoon fresh lemon juice
Confectioners' sugar

1. Preheat oven to 400°F.

2. Put orange zest in food processor with sugar and mince, or chop finely by hand.

3. Mix zest with flour and spread in pie shell. Arrange rhubarb on top.

4. Cover pie loosely with foil and bake 40 to 45 minutes, or until fruit is just tender. (It will continue cooking for a few minutes after it is removed from the oven.) Set aside to cool.

5. Place raspberries decoratively on top in concentric circles. Heat raspberry preserves with water and lemon juice, and when almost cool, paint tops of raspberries with a pastry brush, covering all nooks and crannies, to achieve an even glaze.

6. Just before serving, dust lightly with sifted confectioners' sugar. If desired, serve with vanilla ice cream or a bowl of lightly whipped cream.

Working time: 40 minutes
Preparation time: 2 hours
Serves 6–8

◆

DEEP-DISH PLUM PIE

This is an old family favorite. The wonderful Italian prune plums available in the fall are superb when cooked. They are very juicy and should not be cooked in a two-crust pie. This dessert needs to be served carefully in bowls with spoons so that each serving consists of plums and juice topped with pie crust that has not been dunked in the juices.

¾ cup sugar
1 tablespoon cinnamon
½ tablespoon cornstarch (optional)
6 cups small freestone plums
3 tablespoons butter, cut in small pieces

Flaky Pie Pastry (page 90)

1. Generously butter a 1½-quart heat-proof baking dish, and preheat oven to 400°F.

2. Mix sugar, cinnamon, and cornstarch, if desired. (Cornstarch will

thicken juices slightly.)

3. Cut plums in half — or in quarters if they are very large — and remove pits. Fill baking dish with layers of plums; on top of each layer sprinkle sugar mixture and scatter a few bits of butter. End with a layer of the sugar mixture.

4. Cover plums with a single layer of pastry. Crimp edges and bake for about 35 minutes, or until juices have bubbled up and the crust is a nice golden brown. Serve warm.

NOTE: Place baking dish on a baking sheet, because the juices may overflow and burn in your oven.

Working time: 25 minutes
Preparation time: 1 hour
Serves 8

◆

WARM PEAR TART

During the fall pear season, it is particularly nice to have a warm dessert. This one is a bit time-consuming and is best when served right out of the oven, but it can be prepared immediately before you sit down to dinner and served still slightly warm, if necessary (see photograph on page 35). Be sure to use a tart pan with a removable bottom.

CRUST PASTRY

1 cup flour, plus extra for dusting
½ cup cold butter, cut in small pieces
2 tablespoons ice water,
   approximately

FILLING

3 or 4 pears — Bosc, Bartlett, or other
6 tablespoons apricot jam or apple
   jelly, melted and thinned with 1

tablespoon water
2 tablespoons butter, in small pieces
3 tablespoons sugar
Whipped cream, for garnish (optional)

1. Put flour and butter in a food processor, and pulse machine on and off until mixture looks like coarse bread crumbs.

2. With machine off, add water. Pulse the machine a few times, until the

dough starts to form several balls. Do not blend it into one big mass.

3. Put pastry on a lightly floured board, and dust top with a little flour. With your fingers, gather pastry into a ball. Chill in refrigerator for 20 minutes.

4. Roll out dough, handling as little as possible, into a 14-inch circle. Fold pastry gently in half to transfer to a fluted 12-inch tart pan, then unfold. Fit into pan. Trim edges so they are slightly larger than pan, and fold them back into pan between circle of dough and pan sides. Press pastry against sides of pan with your fingers, smoothing to an even thickness all around.

5. Put tart pastry in refrigerator to chill for another 20 minutes. Preheat oven to 400°F. Place an empty baking sheet on bottom rack of oven to get very hot while you prepare filling.

6. Peel, core, and halve pears lengthwise. Place on their flat side and cut into the thinnest possible slices, starting at thick end. Lay slices in concentric overlapping circles in the tart shell, starting at outside edge of tart and ending in center, in a pattern similar to a fully opened rose.

7. Paint pears with jam or jelly glaze, dot with butter, and sprinkle with sugar.

8. Place tart on hot cookie sheet on lowest shelf of 400°F. oven and bake for 6 minutes, then move it to top shelf and bake another 6 to 8 minutes, or until edges of pears start to brown. Watch carefully to avoid burning.

9. Allow to cool for a few minutes, then remove pan sides and serve on bottom tin, placed on serving plate. Garnish with whipped cream, if desired.

Working time: 1 hour
Preparation time: 1½ hours
Serves 8

◆

RASPBERRY OR STRAWBERRY TARTS

A bright red dessert is always festive. Fresh, perfectly ripe strawberries or raspberries, glazed and arranged in a large tart pastry or in individual shells, are always a favorite and make tarts that are suitable for any occasion.

2 pints fresh raspberries or
    strawberries
8 ounces cream cheese (not whipped)
¼ cup sifted confectioners' sugar
2 tablespoons heavy cream
10-inch Short Crust Pastry shell
    (page 91), prebaked
1 8-ounce jar currant jelly or 1 recipe
    Raspberry Sauce (page 181)
Chopped green pistachios or almonds
Whipped cream

1. If using strawberries, rinse them very quickly under running water and immediately turn out onto dish towel and pat dry. Hull berries.

2. Mix cream cheese with confectioners' sugar and cream.

3. Spread cream cheese mixture in tart shell, and top with berries arranged in concentric circles.

4. Melt currant jelly with a little water in a saucepan, and brush on berries with a pastry brush.

5. Sprinkle chopped nuts over top. Serve at once, accompanied by whipped cream.

NOTE: If there are extra berries, mash them with a little sugar and strain, then spread the puree on the cheese mixture before the berries. Or mix the strained juice with a little sugar and cornstarch (see recipe for Raspberry Sauce) and use to glaze the berries instead of the jelly or Raspberry Sauce.

Working time: 15 minutes
Preparation time: 15 minutes
Serves 6–8

◆

SAND TARTS

Tart tins come in all shapes and sizes. These tarts are usually made in miniature tins about 1½ inches in diameter. When filled with a colorful variety of fillings, they make a pretty addition to the buffet or a tea tray (see photograph on page 87). The pastry is too strong to use for large tarts; you cannot cut it with a knife.

1 cup butter
1 cup sugar
1 egg
1 teaspoon vanilla extract
2½ cups flour
Filling of choice: Lemon Curd (page 187), custard and glazed fruit, jam, or fruit mousse

1. With an electric mixer, cream butter, then add sugar and beat well. Add egg, then vanilla and flour. Mix well. Chill dough.

2. Preheat oven to 375°F.

3. Pinch off small amounts of dough, fit each into a small tart shell, and smooth dough against sides as carefully as possible. Dough should be quite thin and smooth. Remove any excess from top edges.

4. Place tins on a baking sheet and bake for 15 minutes. Cool before removing tarts from tins.

5. Fill shells at last moment and serve at once.

Working time: 45 minutes
Preparation time: 2 hours
Makes 50 small tarts

◆

ULTIMATE PUMPKIN TART

Pumpkin has a wonderful affinity for molasses and rum. This new twist on an old Thanksgiving favorite can easily become a tradition. As an alternative, use a short crust pastry shell and omit the nuts from the topping. It is important to use good-quality molasses and flavorful pumpkin.

NUT CRUST PASTRY

2 cups flour
1½ teaspoons grated orange zest
¼ teaspoon salt
½ teaspoon cinnamon
½ teaspoon nutmeg
¾ cup cold butter, cut into small
    pieces
1 cup ground pecans or walnuts
⅔ cup light brown sugar, packed
2 egg yolks
3 to 5 tablespoons cold orange juice

PUMPKIN FILLING

2½ cups pureed pumpkin, preferably
    fresh
⅔ cup light brown sugar, packed
½ cup dark unsulphured molasses
½ teaspoon ground cloves
¼ teaspoon allspice
¼ teaspoon nutmeg
1 teaspoon cinnamon
1 teaspoon ground ginger
3 eggs
⅓ cup brandy or rum
1 tablespoon cornstarch
⅔ cup heavy cream

MOLASSES TOPPING

¾ cup light brown sugar, packed
3 tablespoons dark unsulphured
    molasses

4 tablespoons butter
1 cup coarsely chopped pecans or
    walnuts

1. Make crust. Mix flour, orange zest, salt, cinnamon, and nutmeg in a mixer or food processor.

2. Add butter pieces and process briefly until mixture resembles coarse meal. (If you are using an electric mixer, cut butter in by hand with a pastry blender.)

3. Add nuts, brown sugar, and egg yolks, and mix only enough to blend.

4. Add just enough orange juice to make dough come together. Wrap dough in plastic film and refrigerate dough until firm, about 30 minutes.

5. Roll out dough to a ¼-inch thickness. Line a 2-inch-high, 10- to 12 inch tart or springform pan. Trim dough and cover with foil. Refrigerate at least 1 hour, or overnight.

6. Preheat oven to 425°F. Make filling. In an electric mixer, mix pumpkin puree, brown sugar, molasses, spices, and eggs.

7. Mix brandy or rum with cornstarch, and add to pumpkin mixture. Whip cream until stiff and fold into pumpkin mixture.

8. Pour filling into tart shell and bake for 15 minutes. Turn oven down to

350°F. and bake for about 1 hour, or until filling is puffed and firm to touch. It should have the consistency of a cheesecake.

9. Cool slowly, out of a draft, until lukewarm. Tart may be left to cool in a turned-off oven.

10. Make the topping. Preheat broiler. Mix all ingredients together and heat in a saucepan, then pour over cooled tart. Place tart under broiler, and heat until topping is bubbly and thoroughly melted, about 3 minutes. Do not burn.

11. Remove sides of tart pan and serve tart at room temperature, accompanied by whipped cream.

NOTE: Avoid putting the tart in the refrigerator before serving, as the topping will get sugary.

Working time: 1 hour
Preparation time: 2 hours
Serves 8–10

◆

INDIVIDUAL CHESS PIES

Chess pies are a good choice for a dessert buffet, for taking on picnics, or for giving as a gift. They keep best when frozen.

CRUST PASTRY

⅔ cup butter, chilled
2 cups flour
¼ cup ice water, approximately

RAISIN FILLING

2 cups raisins
2 cups light brown sugar, packed
1 cup butter
6 egg yolks
2 cups coarsely chopped walnut meats
1 teaspoon vanilla extract
Spiced Whipped Cream (page 182)

1. Preheat oven to 425°F.

2. Blend butter into flour with a pastry blender or a food processor until it is the consistency of coarse meal.

3. Add water 1 tablespoon at a time until you can make a ball with your fingers. Keep dough as dry as possible and do not handle very much. Chill for 15 minutes.

4. Roll out pastry on a floured surface until ⅛ inch thick. Using a cookie cutter larger than cups of a miniature muffin tin, cut pastry into rounds. Fit 1 round into each cup in muffin tin. Press dough into cup, and trim edges.

5. Pour a little hot water over raisins and let soak for a few minutes. Drain.

6. Cream brown sugar and butter. Add egg yolks, raisins, nuts, and vanilla. Spoon mixture into muffin cups.

7. Bake for 5 minutes, then reduce heat to 300°F. and bake until brown and bubbly on top. Serve with Spiced Whipped Cream.

VARIATIONS: 1. Add ½ cup brandy or bourbon to filling and increase baking time by 5 minutes. 2. Use mincemeat to which liqueur has been added instead of raisins. 3. Use this filling for a whole 10-inch pie and bake until filling is crusty and set, about 35 minutes.

Working time: 1 hour
Preparation time: approximately 1½ hours
Serves about 16

◆

APPLE TART TATIN

This dessert is a bit difficult to master but well worth the effort. The easiest mistake you can make is to undercook it, since then the tart will not hold its shape when inverted. It will still taste good, but the cook's pride may suffer. Two and a half hours is a long time to bake any pastry, and if you double the recipe it

will take longer still. Slip a piece of foil over the top midway through the baking if the crust starts to brown too quickly. Do not cool the tart too long in the pan or the apples will stick to the bottom. Any leftovers are delicious chilled.

FILLING

4 large Granny Smith or other firm,
    tart apples
⅓ cup butter, at room temperature
1¾ cups sugar
1 to 4 tablespoons fresh lemon juice
    (optional)

CRUST PASTRY

1 cup cold butter
1⅓ cups flour
1 tablespoon sugar
4 to 5 tablespoons ice water, as needed

TO FINISH

1 cup vanilla-flavored whipped cream,
    for garnish

1. Peel, core, and slice apples ⅛ inch thick. Do not chop them.

2. Butter 2 pieces of aluminum foil 2 inches wide and long enough to stretch across pan and up sides with extra left on each side. Lay them in pan at right angles.

3. Spread ½ butter on bottom and sides of a heavy baking or frying pan, about 10 inches in diameter and 2 to 4 inches deep. (Lined copper works well.) The bottom requires a thicker coating of butter than sides. Apples will caramelize better if you use a metal pan, but you can see when juices are gone if you use a glass pan.

4. Sprinkle about ⅓ sugar on buttered pan bottom. Melt remaining butter. Place a layer of most neatly sliced apples in an overlapping pattern on bottom and up sides of dish. Paint with melted butter and sprinkle lightly with sugar. Then add more layers of apples, painting each layer with butter and sprinkling with sugar until dish is absolutely full. Use extra butter and sugar if you run out. (The center will collapse a bit as it cooks and as the liquid evaporates.) If apples are not tart, squeeze lemon juice on each layer to taste. Finish with melted butter. Press down firmly in pan. Set aside while making crust.

5. Preheat oven to 350°F.

6. Cut butter for crust into small bits.

7. Sift flour with sugar. Cut or rub

butter into flour with a pastry blender or your fingertips until it makes a fine meal, or put in a food processor and pulse.

8. Sprinkle with ice water, using only as much as is necessary to form a ball. Place dough on a well-floured board. Pat — do not roll — ball of dough into a circle about 11 inches in diameter, or a little larger than your pan. Turn dough over several times as you shape it so that it will not stick to board. Handle as little as possible; it need not be smooth.

9. Lay dough over apples, folding edges of dough in between pan and apples. Press dough against sides of pan firmly but gently, so it is securely in place. Cut a few small holes in dough with a sharp, pointed knife.

10. Bake for 2 to 2½ hours! Apples must caramelize and all juices evaporate or tart will not unmold correctly. If crust browns too quickly, cover it loosely with a sheet of aluminum foil. Check to be sure juices are evaporated by tipping pan before removing it from oven.

11. Let tart cool about 5 minutes, then invert pan over a large, flat, round serving plate. Remove aluminum foil strips. Let tart continue cooling. It will taste best 45 minutes after it comes out of oven, but it can be made several hours before serving time. Serve with whipped cream as garnish.

N O T E: Unmolding a tart tatin can be tricky. If necessary, loosen the sides with a thin spatula, and break the surface tension on the bottom by gently tugging at the strips of foil after the tart is inverted onto the serving platter and before the pan is removed.

Working time: 45 minutes
Preparation time: 4 hours
Serves about 8

◆

BLUEBERRY TART

This recipe can also be used for any fruit that is desirable to keep almost raw, such as strawberries and raspberries. The amount of sugar and the necessity for cornstarch will depend on the fruit selected.

I keep some unfilled baked pie crusts in my freezer at all times so they are handy for this quick and easy dessert. Either flaky or short crust pastry shells are good choices.

---

4 cups fresh blueberries
1¾ cups sugar
2 tablespoons cornstarch
¾ cup water
Juice and grated zest of about 1 lemon
Cinnamon (optional)
1 10- or 12-inch Short Crust Pastry
   shell (page 91), prebaked

1. Wash berries, lay on a towel, and pat with another towel to dry thoroughly.

2. Mix sugar and cornstarch with a fork and add cold water. Mix well.

3. Put cornstarch mixture in a pan and add 1 cup blueberries, lemon juice, and zest. Cook until blueberries are thoroughly smashed and syrup is clear. Strain through a fine strainer. Mixture should be thick, transparent, and glossy. Let cool and then taste for flavor. Cinnamon can be added if mixture is bland.

4. Add remaining berries and stir gently so all are coated.

5. Pour berries into tart shell and smooth top. There should be enough syrup so a fairly smooth surface results and all berries are coated. Do not refrigerate; serve within 2 hours.

Working time: 20 minutes
Preparation time: 1 hour
Serves 8

◆

MERINGUES

Baked Alaska (page 118)

Meringue is a simple mixture of egg white and sugar. Few chemical components, when mixed in a laboratory, produce such spectacular results. With the addition of heat and air, the mixture reaches enormous volume and achieves a shiny white surface, a smooth and thick texture, and a silken sweet flavor.

The origin of meringues is in dispute, but they first became popular in France through Marie Antoinette, who enjoyed them so much that she made them herself at the Trianon Palace. It was not until the nineteenth century that the great chef Carême first piped meringue into decorative shapes.

My fascination with meringues began in the Rocky Mountains, where as a child I was the friend of a lovely old lady who used to make them for me. In those times electric mixers were a very new thing and even hand beaters were absent from many kitchens. My friend simply put the egg whites on a white porcelain platter and, with an ordinary table fork, pulled and lifted them in a circular fashion until air was incorporated and they rose into snowy peaks. Sugar was slowly added and eventually the mounds were firmed up in a wood stove. The next day the special delights were ready to eat — soft, crumbly, and just slightly chewy in the middle. Because the process took so long, it was a very special thing to watch, and it allowed me time to contemplate the magic. Try this technique sometime; it will give you a lighter result, bigger arm muscles, and a new appreciation for the modern appliances and kitchen gadgets we take for granted.

TECHNIQUES

One of the most important ingredients of many desserts, egg whites have to be handled with great care. They will not elevate properly if a trace of grease, moisture, or egg yolk is present. Always make sure your bowl is thoroughly clean and dry. It is better not to wipe it with a dish towel, since the towel might contain traces of grease. I try to reserve a bowl exclusively for beating egg whites, and I always wash and dry it in the dishwasher. Ditto for the beaters.

It is easier to achieve volume with egg whites that are at room temperature (65–90°F.) and at least 3 days old — no worry with store-bought eggs. Separated egg whites can be kept in tightly covered glass jars in the refrigerator for several days, or even for a couple of weeks if they came straight to you from the chicken. Copper bowls give greater volume; plastic bowls should never be used, since it is almost impossible to ensure that they are free of grease. Fine whisks with many wires are preferable to coarse ones. Half a lemon can be rubbed on the bowl before beating if grease is suspected. I add a quarter teaspoon of cream of tartar per 4 egg whites to ensure stability, whether or not a recipe calls for it.

Sugar must be added very gradually, and only when the whites have achieved their full volume. Superfine sugar yields by far the best results. Its fine texture has a greater surface area, which allows faster dissolution and prevents its mass from weighing down the egg-white mixture. Meringues from bakeries tend to be made with confectioners' sugar, which results in a very fine-textured, sturdy, and less delicious product.

Always start adding the sugar a tablespoon at a time while beating continuously; as the mixture becomes denser, the sugar can be added more quickly. I always taste as I proceed to determine when enough sugar has been added. The mixture should be about as sweet as marshmallow and should hold its peaks without the tips bending over.

When baking meringues, place the mixture on parchment paper, which insulates it somewhat from the direct heat of the baking sheet and makes it easier to handle after cooling, or use an insulated pan. The parchment can be lightly coated with vegetable oil spray. When making layers for a torte, place a large mound of meringue mixture in the center of a precut circle and spread to the edges with a spatula; the layer should be at least three-quarters of an inch thick. You can also put the mixture in a clean pastry bag and pipe concentric circles onto the paper rounds.

Bake meringues in a very slow oven (200°F.) and leave them in a turned-off oven overnight to dry thoroughly. Bake for about 1 hour, but watch and turn off the oven before any browning occurs. In some ovens that is 10 minutes.

Meringues should be white in color and delicate. They can be stored in airtight containers for several days or in the freezer if they will be used later in a frozen dessert. If a slightly chewier meringue is desired, bake in an oven preheated to 275°F. for less time.

USES

Ordinary meringues are often paired with Crème Chantilly (page 175) or ice cream, or layered and filled with mousse. Meringue mixtures also give body and freezer softness to bombes, sherbets, and mousses, and are a lovely frosting for cakes, pies, and, of course, Baked Alaska (page 118).

Many desserts can be made less fattening and lighter by incorporating beaten egg whites or meringue in addition to or instead of about half the whipped cream specified. Try this substitution in the Raspberry Bavarian Cream Carême (page 27) or Maple Mousse (page 29).

◆
◆
◆

ORDINARY MERINGUE

Meringues are easy, versatile, and fat–free. They are also delicious and lovely to look at, and are a good way to use leftover egg whites.

5 egg whites, at room temperature
¼ teaspoon cream of tartar
1½ cups superfine sugar

1. Preheat oven to 200°F. Line a baking sheet with parchment paper, or grease lightly.

2. Beat egg whites with an electric mixer until soft peaks start to form. While beating, add cream of tartar, then gradually add sugar. After at least half is added, you can increase your speed. The mixture should get stiff and hold its shape when a beater is removed.

3. Spoon meringue onto baking sheet, or pipe decorative shapes or circles with a pastry bag.

4. Bake for about 30 minutes to 1 hour, then shut off oven and leave meringues to dry thoroughly, at least 3 hours. If you like a chewier meringue, bake at 275°F. for 15 minutes, then shut off oven.

Working time: 15 minutes
Preparation time: 4 hours
Serves 12

◆

ALMOND MERINGUE

This meringue mixture can be used to make individual meringues. It is also possible to use finely ground hazelnuts, pecans, or cashews, but the flavor will not be as delicate. The baked layers can be wrapped and frozen and will make a good emergency dessert when filled with layers of fruit and whipped cream or various flavors of ice cream.

5 egg whites
¼ teaspoon cream of tartar
1 cup superfine sugar
1½ cups blanched ground almonds

1. Adjust oven rack to its lowest position. Preheat oven to 200°F.

2. Whip egg whites to soft peaks, add cream of tartar, and gradually add sugar, beating until whites are shiny and firm. Fold in ground almonds.

3. Make parchment circles ½ inch smaller in diameter than your soufflé dish (there should be 2–3 disks per dish). Place parchment circles on a baking sheet. Pipe or spread a layer of meringue at least ⅝ inch thick on each circle.

4. Bake until meringues just start to color, about 15 minutes, then turn off oven and allow the meringues to cool for 4 hours or overnight.

NOTE: Leftover uncooked meringue can be baked as individual cookies. Leftover cooked meringue may be crumbled and mixed with whipped cream and served over ice cream or cut-up fruit.

Working time: 15 minutes
Preparation time: 4 hours
Makes three 10-inch disks

◆

SPANISH WIND TORTE, OR VACHERIN

A Spanish Wind Torte, or Vacherin, is a hollow container of meringue that is filled with fruit, ice cream, or mousse. It is fun and impressive. If the art of making meringues is mastered, this torte is only a matter of mastering the use of a pastry bag to decorate. It is possible to reuse the meringue container if you serve the contents with individual meringues and line the Vacherin with foil. Or, if it is on the buffet, you can choose not to fill it and just have it as decoration.

Double recipe of Ordinary Meringue (page 112), in 3 batches
1 quart fruit, ice cream, or mousse

1. Preheat oven to 200°F. Cut 5 parchment paper circles with diameters of about 9 inches each, and lay them on baking sheets.

2. Using first batch of meringue, spread meringue on one of the circles, covering it entirely with a layer about 1 inch thick. This is the bottom. On 3 more circles, pipe a ring of meringue about 1 inch wide at outside edge. On fifth circle, draw a smaller circle about 6½ inches in diameter. Cover this smaller circle completely with meringue.

3. Bake all circles for about 30 minutes, then leave to dry in turned-off oven for at least 3 hours.

4. Preheat oven to 200°F. Assemble the layers, using second batch of meringue. Place bottom layer on a baking sheet and place a ring on top, gluing them together with meringue. Glue other rings on top, then spread an even layer of meringue over outside, filling in all cracks between layers. Do the same on inside of container. Rebake for 30 minutes, then allow to dry for at least 3 hours in turned-off oven.

5. Preheat oven to 200°F. With third batch of meringue, pipe arabesques and other designs over outside and top. Bake again for 20 to 30 minutes, watching very carefully so there is absolutely no browning. Leave oven door propped open if necessary to keep the heat low. Leave in turned-off oven for at least 6 hours to dry.

6. Fill and serve Vacherin, or place in a

plastic bag, seal, and keep in a dry place until ready to use. Although the torte will retain its looks indefinitely, it will taste best if used when freshly made.

NOTE: Some cooks prefer the toasted look of a Baked Alaska. If you do, increase the baking time in each step to brown the meringues to desired color.

Working time: 2 hours
Preparation time: 2 days
Serves 12

◆

APRICOT MERINGUE TORTE

This torte is very adaptable. Many children who are not cake lovers think this is a super birthday cake. It is far less fuss to make; and if you are in a hurry, you can cheat and put apricot jam between the layers instead of pureed apricots. It is also very good made with prunes or fresh raspberries.

Apricot Mousse (page 23)
3 10-inch Meringue Layers, Ordinary or Almond (pages 112, 113)
Crème Chantilly (page 175)
Chocolate Curls or Leaves (pages 200, 201)

1. Put half Apricot Mousse on top of one meringue layer, then place second meringue layer over filling and spread remaining Apricot Mousse on top. Place third meringue layer on top, flat side up.

2. Spread a heavy layer of Crème Chantilly on top and decorate with the Chocolate Curls or Leaves. Refrigerate until ready to serve.

Working time: 50 minutes
Preparation time: 2 hours
Serves 10

◆

FROZEN PRALINE MERINGUE

This dessert can be prepared ahead. Freeze it uncovered and then wrap it carefully, or the whipped cream will take on tastes from the freezer. Do not allow the dessert to defrost for too long — like ice cream, it should be served chilled and must never come to room temperature.

5 egg whites
⅛ teaspoon cream of tartar
1½ cups superfine sugar
1½ cups sliced blanched almonds
1 pint vanilla ice cream
3 cups heavy cream
¼ cup sifted confectioners' sugar
1½ tablespoons dark rum
Candied violets or rose petals,
    for decoration

1. Preheat oven to 200°F. Select a soufflé dish about 10 inches in diameter. Spray nonstick coating on two 18 × 12-inch baking sheets. Cut two 9½-inch parchment circles and place them on baking sheet.

2. In a large mixing bowl, beat egg whites until stiff but not dry. Add cream of tartar and gradually beat in 1 cup of superfine sugar until stiff peaks form. (Some sugar should remain slightly granular to make a very tender meringue.)

3. Fill a pastry bag fitted with a round nozzle. Pipe or spread a layer of meringue at least ⅝ inch thick on each parchment circle. Bake meringues for about 30 minutes or until hard, then turn oven off without opening door. Leave meringues in oven for at least 5 hours. The meringues may be light beige in color.

4. Lightly oil a large baking sheet. In a heavy, medium saucepan, cook remaining ½ cup superfine sugar over a moderately high heat, stirring occasionally with a wooden spoon as the sugar closest to sides of pan begins to melt. Stir melting sugar into dry sugar in center. After 6 to 7 minutes, mixture will turn a rich caramel color. Add almonds; this will solidify caramel slightly. Continue cooking to remelt sugar and brown almonds, about 2 minutes longer. Pour praline onto oiled sheet and let cool.

5. Let ice cream soften slightly. Mean-

ENTERTAINING DESSERTS

while, break praline into pieces and process in a food processor until finely ground. Scoop softened ice cream into a large bowl and, with a rubber spatula, fold in powdered praline. Firm ice cream slightly in freezer.

6. In a large bowl, combine cream, confectioners' sugar, and rum. Beat with an electric mixer until stiff. Cover and refrigerate until needed.

7. If necessary, carefully trim meringues so they fit a 10-inch soufflé dish and reserve trimmings. Put a thin layer of ice cream in the bottom of soufflé dish, then a meringue disk and a layer of whipped cream. Fill soufflé dish with a remaining layer of ice cream, the second meringue disk, and some whipped cream. Sprinkle any crumbled meringue trimmings over top and freeze until very firm.

8. Unmold dessert and spread additional whipped cream on sides and top for a smooth finish. Spoon remaining whipped cream into a pastry bag fitted with a star tip. Decorate top and the base of cake with whipped-cream rosettes. Gently press candied violets or rose petals into rosettes and place dessert, uncovered, in freezer. Freeze for at least 3 hours, or until hard. You can also serve it from soufflé dish.

9. Cover cake with plastic wrap and 2 layers of aluminum foil, and return to the freezer. About 30 minutes before serving time, unwrap cake and transfer to refrigerator to soften slightly before cutting and serving.

Working time: 1 hour
Preparation time: 5 hours
Serves 12

◆

BAKED ALASKA

Although this is a relatively simple version, Baked Alaska is always impressive. Endless variations are possible. If you do not plan to refreeze the cake after assembly, it is nice to impregnate it with some liqueur and separate the ice cream and cake with cut-up fresh fruit, such as peaches or strawberries. Whatever your method, the ice cream should always be frozen very stiff when it goes into the oven, so it won't melt (see photograph on page 109).

Any good sponge cake will work; if you are short on time, a store-bought pound cake makes a pretty good base. Alternatively, make a double recipe of Cookie Crumb Crust (page 92), form it into the correct shape, about ½ inch thick, and bake for 10 minutes, then use in place of the cake. The important thing is to insulate the ice cream on all sides.

1 Genoise (page 48)
2 quarts ice cream
5 egg whites, at room temperature
½ teaspoon cream of tartar
1 cup superfine sugar, or more
Sauce of choice

1. Cut cake to fit bottom of mold you plan to use. Place it on a foil-covered breadboard or on heavy cardboard, not on a metal dish. Set aside.

2. Soften ice cream and fill mold with it, packing it in tightly. Freeze again.

3. Preheat oven to 400°F. In a very clean bowl, beat egg whites with cream of tartar until medium-firm peaks are formed. Gradually add sugar, at first very slowly, while continuing to beat at high speed. The mixture should get stiffer and stiffer as more sugar is added. When very stiff peaks are formed and all sugar is incorporated, unmold ice cream onto the top of cake. Spread an even layer of meringue over ice cream and cake, making sure there are no gaps.

4. Put remainder of meringue in a pastry bag with a large decorative tip and pipe arabesques, scrolls, or whatever you wish all over meringue. The average depth of the meringue should be ¾ to 1 inch.

5. Place Baked Alaska immediately in oven and bake until all meringue tips are nicely browned. Serve at once with a sauce complementary to your flavor of ice cream.

NOTE: Cake may be held for several hours in freezer before baking.

To serve this dessert flaming, there are two techniques: 1. Using a small piece of foil, make a depression in the meringue before baking to hold the foil in a cup shape. Just before bringing the dessert to the table, fill the foil with warmed brandy and ignite. The brandy may then be spooned onto each slice as it is served. 2. Place the Baked Alaska on a heavy nonmetallic serving platter, and then spoon warmed brandy around the edge and light it. This may cause some singeing of the meringue but the resulting dessert is more impressive.

Working time: 20 minutes
Preparation time: 1½ hours
Serves 12

◆

GINGER FLOATING ISLAND WITH RASPBERRY SAUCE

This dessert is not as difficult as it may seem (see photograph on page 171). The custard can be made the day before, and the meringue in the morning of the day that it will be served. The dessert is quickly assembled, but remember that all the parts must chill for 1 hour before serving. I sometimes add ¼ cup of good-quality ginger marmalade to the meringue in place of some of the sugar.

CUSTARD SAUCE

8 egg yolks
½ cup sugar
2 cups milk or light cream
1 teaspoon vanilla extract

FLOATING ISLAND

8 egg whites
¾ cup superfine sugar
½ cup finely chopped crystallized ginger
Raspberry Sauce (page 181)

1. Prepare custard sauce. Beat egg yolks with sugar until they are pale yellow and thick enough to fall in ribbons from whisk.

2. In a large, heavy saucepan, bring milk to a boil. Remove from heat and skim off any skin that has formed. Stir in vanilla, then gradually whisk about 1 cup hot milk into beaten egg yolks to warm them gently. Whisk yolks back into milk in saucepan. Cook over low heat, stirring constantly, until custard thickens enough to coat the back of a wooden spoon, about 10 minutes.

3. Strain custard into a bowl set in a larger bowl of ice cubes. Stir to cool custard to room temperature quickly, about 5 minutes. (If you use a metal bowl, it will facilitate the cooling process.) Remove custard from ice and set it aside, stirring occasionally to prevent a skin from forming. (The custard sauce may be made ahead to this point. Cover surface of custard with buttered plastic wrap to prevent a skin from forming, and refrigerate. Stir before using.)

4. Prepare meringue. Preheat oven to 350°F. Butter and sugar a tall 6-cup mold.

5. In a large mixing bowl, beat egg whites until stiff peaks form. Gradually add sugar, beating constantly,

until meringue is shiny and thick. Gently fold in ginger.

6. Turn meringue into mold and lightly cover with buttered parchment or wax paper. Place mold in a roasting pan or large casserole and pour in enough hot water to reach ¾ of the way up sides of mold. Place in lower third of the oven and bake for 30 to 40 minutes, or until meringue is firm to the touch and begins to shrink away from sides of mold. It will rise about 3 inches and brown on top.

7. Remove mold from water bath and let cool to room temperature. (This may be done in the morning, but do not refrigerate.) Unmold meringue onto a large round platter about 1 hour before serving.

8. To assemble, place meringue in a serving bowl and pour about 1½ cups of custard sauce around it. Pour about ¾ cup of the Raspberry Sauce on top of meringue, so that a pool forms on top and ribbons of sauce drip down sides. Pour about ½ cup of Raspberry Sauce in a thin circle on top of custard. Draw a knife through raspberry sauce at 2-inch intervals from edge of meringue outward to create a marbled pattern. To serve, pass remaining sauces separately.

NOTE: Be careful when chopping ginger. If you use a food proces-sor, it may permanently abrade the bowl.

Working time: 1 hour
Preparation time: 3 hours
Serves 8

◆

ALMOND MERINGUE CAKE

This unusual flourless cake is quite sweet and goes well with ice cream or sorbet. With lots of piped designs in the meringue, it makes a spectacular birthday cake.

12 eggs, separated
1 pound sifted confectioners' sugar
1 pound unblanched almonds, grated
8-ounce jar currant jelly, melted with
    2 tablespoons water
7-Minute Boiled Icing (page 193) or
    Italian Meringue (page 188)

1. Preheat the oven to 300°F.

2. Beat egg yolks, add ½ confectioners' sugar, and beat well. Fold in ½ almonds.

3. Beat egg whites until stiff peaks form. Add remaining sugar, slowly at first, beating until very thick. Gradually add remaining almonds, combining well.

4. Fold mixtures together carefully, then pour into a 12-inch springform or tube pan, or into 2 or more cake pans. Bake for 1 to 1½ hours, or until tan and slightly springy. Cool overnight in pans, loosely covered.

5. Preheat oven to 400°F. Remove cake from pan. Spread cake with currant jelly, then frost with icing or meringue. If making layers, spread currant jelly on bottom layer and

cover with top layer, then spread remaining currant jelly on top, and then frost. Place in oven, on rack near bottom, and toast until a delicate shade of brown, about 5 to 8 minutes.

NOTE: A nice variation is to fill the Almond Meringue layers with prune puree. First, cook some dried prunes, drain them, puree them, then sweeten to taste and flavor with brandy. Use this puree to fill the layers, then glaze the top and sides of the cake with Apricot Glaze (page 194) instead of currant jelly before frosting with meringue.

Working time: 1 hour
Preparation time: 1 day
Serves 12
◆

CHAPTER 6

SOUFFLES: HOT, COLD, AND FROZEN

Hot Chocolate Soufflé (page 129)

Soufflés are simple mixtures of eggs and flavorings. They derive their lightness from the air that is beaten into the egg whites. Because egg whites have the ability to hold air, when the mixture is cooked each little air bubble expands, making the total mixture grow to even taller proportions. On the other hand, cold soufflés are not cooked and must get their lightness from beaten egg whites and whipped cream.

A hot chocolate soufflé, rising over the edge of the dish, with a cracked crust dusted with confectioners' sugar and a soft bottom, is not only pleasing to the eye but immensely satisfying to the cook.

TECHNIQUES

The basis of a typical hot soufflé is a mixture of butter and flour (a roux), added to milk, cooked until thick, and then added to beaten egg yolks and flavorings. When the egg yolk mixture has cooled to room temperature, it can be folded into the beaten whites and baked. There is a difference of opinion, however, on the advisability of cooking the egg yolks before incorporating them into the beaten whites. Generally I add the egg yolks to the milk base and cook the mixture, but that is not essential. I have discovered that what really matters is that the egg yolk mixture be of roughly the same thickness as the whites or the latter will deflate when being folded in. The egg whites may be at room temperature or colder, but cold whites take more time to beat.

The steps are simple: (1) Melt butter, add the flour mixed with sugar, then add all the milk, stirring so lumps will break up. (2) Cook the mixture until very hot, then add, a little at a time, to the egg yolks until all is incorporated. Reheat gently until the mixture becomes thicker than custard. (3) Cool the mixture to room temperature. (4) Beat the egg whites until stiff and fold the yolk mixture into the whites. (5) Pour into a straight-sided soufflé dish that has been greased and sugared. Bake as directed in recipe.

HINTS

Soufflés can be held unbaked in the refrigerator for as long as 1 hour before baking, but if refrigerated after mixing, the baking time will have to be increased. This allows you to finish the dish completely before company arrives and simply slip it into the oven when sitting down to dinner.

A straight-sided dish is essential to give soufflé mixtures something to cling to as they rise. Most dessert soufflés are baked with the bottom of the dish resting in a pan of hot water so that the soufflé's bottom will be barely cooked and can act as a sauce for the drier top. If you like the whole soufflé to be light and airy, omit this step.

Soufflés fall when they are exposed to a rapid change of temperature, when they are not cooked enough, or when they are not served immediately. Before removing a soufflé from the oven, have a serving plate ready and the guests' plates in front of them.

To make a very high soufflé, use a piece of aluminum foil several layers thick to make a collar around the dish. Tape or tie it tightly to the outside of the dish, so it stands up at least 2 inches above the edge. Grease and sugar the collar as well as the dish. When the soufflé is removed from the oven, remove the collar with great care. Run a knife between the collar and the soufflé, then peel it away slowly and carefully.

Should you have the bad luck to have your soufflé fall, you should present it as a hot pudding. No one need know that it was supposed to be a soufflé!

Do not try to make a very large soufflé—6-egg soufflés are the maximum practical. If you have many mouths to feed, make several smaller soufflés or individual ones, which are easier to control.

When making cold soufflés, add a bit of unflavored gelatin to help stabilize the mixture, since egg whites won't hold their air indefinitely. Frozen soufflés are easier than hot ones, and if they are made with a collar, they look pretty. They should be taken from the freezer and placed in the refrigerator about 30 minutes before serving to improve the texture and for ease of serving.

See Chapter 5 introduction for hints on handling egg whites.

HOT LEMON SOUFFLÉ

Lemon is a wonderful palate refresher, and this soufflé is very good after a rich dinner. Beginners need not fear; even a fallen lemon soufflé can be served. Simply call it Hot Lemon Pudding. This recipe can be doubled.

1 cup sugar
2 tablespoons flour
2 tablespoons butter
Juice and zest of 2 lemons
1 cup milk
3 eggs, separated
¼ teaspoon vanilla extract

1. Preheat oven to 350°F. Butter and sugar a 1½-quart soufflé dish.

2. In top of a double boiler, mix sugar with flour. Add butter, lemon juice and zest, and milk. Cook over low heat, stirring continuously until thickened, about 8 minutes.

3. Lightly beat yolks until foamy. Add a bit of hot mixture to egg yolks, then combine in double boiler and cook over hot water another minute, stirring continuously until it starts to thicken. Remove from heat and allow to cool to room temperature.

4. Beat egg whites until they form stiff peaks, then fold lukewarm lemon mixture into whites. Add vanilla and pour into soufflé dish. Set dish in a pan with at least 1 inch of hot water. Bake for about 25 to 30 minutes, or until top is browned, dry, and risen. Avoid opening door more than a crack during cooking.

Working time: 15 minutes
Preparation time: 1 hour
Serves 3–4

◆

HOT CHOCOLATE SOUFFLÉ

Of the many recipes for chocolate soufflé I have tried, I find this to be the best. Soufflés are a personal thing, and I like them to be puffed and dry on the top, and runny and half-cooked on the bottom (see photograph on page 123). If you like your soufflé cooked all the way through, bake it without setting the dish in warm water.

If necessary, this soufflé can be assembled and held in the refrigerator for up to 1 hour before baking. The baking time will have to be increased to about 1 hour if the soufflé starts off cold instead of at room temperature.

2 ounces unsweetened chocolate
3 tablespoons butter
⅓ cup flour
½ cup sugar
1 cup heavy cream
3 eggs, separated
1 teaspoon vanilla extract
Lightly sweetened whipped cream

1. Preheat oven to 350°F. Butter and sugar a 1½-quart soufflé dish.

2. Melt chocolate in top of a double boiler over hot water. Set aside to cool.

3. Melt butter over low heat. Add flour and sugar all at once, and stir until smooth. Add to chocolate.

4. Add cream and stir over low heat until thick. Add a bit of hot mixture to well-beaten egg yolks, then combine and cook over hot water for another minute, stirring continuously.

5. Cool mixture to lukewarm. Beat whites until stiff peaks form, then fold into chocolate mixture and add vanilla.

6. Pour into soufflé dish and set dish in a pan containing at least 1 inch of hot water. Bake for about 35 minutes, or until top has risen and looks dry. (Baking time depends on degree of doneness preferred.)

7. Serve with whipped cream, passed separately.

Working time: 15 minutes
Preparation time: 1 hour
Serves 3–4

◆

COLD CHOCOLATE SOUFFLÉ

This Cold Chocolate Soufflé does not hold well, so do not make it more than a few hours before you plan to serve it.

4 ounces semisweet chocolate
5 tablespoons water
½ tablespoon unflavored gelatin
4 whole eggs
3 egg yolks
4 tablespoons sugar
½ cup slivered almonds

1. Melt chocolate in a pan with 2 tablespoons of water.

2. Soften gelatin in remaining 3 tablespoons water, then dissolve in top of a double boiler over very hot water, stirring constantly until thoroughly melted. Add to chocolate mixture, and allow to cool.

3. Beat eggs, yolks, and sugar in a double boiler over, not touching, simmering water until thick. Remove from heat and add chocolate mixture.

4. Oil a 6-inch band of wax paper or aluminum foil and tie it around a 1½-quart soufflé dish, oiled side in, to form a standing collar.

5. Pour mixture into soufflé dish and refrigerate at least 4 hours.

6. Spread slivered almonds on a baking sheet and toast in a 350°F. oven until medium-tan. Garnish soufflé with almonds. Remove collar and serve.

Working time: 30 minutes
Preparation time: 3 hours
Serves 8

◆

CHAPTER 7

CLASSIC PUDDINGS

American Summer Pudding (page 133)

5. Place a plate just smaller than size of top of bowl over bread. Put a brick, or a heavy stone, on top of plate and press down to compress a bit. Place pudding in refrigerator overnight, or up to 24 hours.

6. When ready to serve, place a deep serving plate over bowl and invert, easing out pudding with plastic strips. Expect extra juice to surround pudding. Serve pudding accompanied by whipped cream.

Working time: 25 minutes
Preparation time: 8–24 hours
Serves 8–10

◆

PINEAPPLE AND RICE PUDDING

Sweet rice dishes are becoming popular again, and it is nice to have a use for fresh pineapple that is so decorative. If only poor-quality pineapples are available, use canned. In this case, use the syrup in the can instead of the brown sugar and water, and caramelize the pineapple very quickly so as not to overcook it. Italian Arborio rice works best, because it doesn't get sticky when it is cooked a long time in liquid.

This dessert is best completed the day before and left in the mold until time to serve it. When ready to unmold, set the bottom of the dish in hot water for a few minutes to loosen the caramel.

PUDDING

1 cup Arborio rice
4 cups water
2⅓ cups milk
½ cup sugar
Zest of 1 orange, cut into ½-inch strips

1 vanilla bean, split in half lengthwise
5 egg yolks
¼ cup butter
1½ tablespoons unflavored gelatin
½ cup Grand Marnier
1 cup heavy cream

ENTERTAINING DESSERTS

PINEAPPLE TOPPING

1 large fresh pineapple

1 cup light brown sugar, packed

⅓ cup water

1. Preheat oven to 350°F. Grease a 12-inch heatproof baking dish or oven-proof skillet.

2. Rinse rice thoroughly under warm water. Bring water to a boil and boil rice for 5 minutes. Drain, rinse in cold water, and drain well. Place in prepared dish.

3. Bring milk, sugar, orange zest, and vanilla bean to a boil in a heavy pan. Pour over rice, cover well, and bake for about 25 to 30 minutes, or until liquid is absorbed. Rice should not get soft or mushy, but rather should be al dente. Remove orange zest and vanilla bean.

4. Cook egg yolks and butter in a double boiler over hot water, stirring constantly until butter is melted and mixture starts to thicken, about 4 minutes. Add hot rice and stir for 2 to 3 minutes until thickened.

5. Soften gelatin in Grand Marnier, and heat it gently until dissolved. Add to rice mixture, then let mixture cool. Meanwhile, beat cream until soft peaks form and fold it into rice. Set aside.

6. Peel and core pineapple. Cut into ⅓-inch crosswise slices to make rings. Set aside.

7. Heat brown sugar and water in a heavy pan until quite thick. Put in pineapple rings and caramelize over high heat, so they brown but do not cook through.

8. Line a straight-sided 10-inch glass dish with 2-inch-high sides with heavy aluminum foil. Butter foil, then place caramelized pineapple in a decorative pattern on bottom, filling any spaces with small pieces so bottom is fairly solid. Use leftover scraps to go up sides, and chill thoroughly.

9. Fill mold with rice mixture, packing in rice so no air spaces are left. Tap mold on table to remove air pockets. Chill for at least 3 hours, then unmold by setting a plate on mold and inverting. Allow to sit for a minute before removing mold so all caramelized juices drip out.

Working time: 1 hour
Preparation time: 5 hours
Serves 10–12

◆

STEAMED CHOCOLATE PUDDING

This is an ideal dessert for a cook who wants to do the cooking ahead and enjoy being with the guests during party time. The pudding can be left in the steaming pot for an extra half-hour without worry. It may even be served lukewarm, but it is definitely better when hot. This is very festive when you make it in a pretty mold.

2 ounces unsweetened chocolate or ¾
    cup cocoa powder
½ cup butter
1 cup sugar
2 eggs, separated
1 cup milk
2 cups flour
2 teaspoons baking powder
Light Chocolate Sauce (page 178)

1. If using chocolate, melt in top of a double boiler over hot water, and allow it to cool to lukewarm.

2. Cream butter and sugar. Beat egg yolks with milk, then add to creamed mixture.

3. Add chocolate or cocoa to creamed mixture, then add 1 cup flour. Beat until smooth.

4. Whip whites until they form stiff peaks, then fold into chocolate mixture. Sift remaining cup of flour with baking powder, and fold into chocolate mixture.

5. Place mixture in a greased 2-quart pudding mold. Cover it loosely with greased foil and place it in a deep pot containing at least 2 inches of water. Support mold so it doesn't touch bottom of pot. (You can sit it on a crumpled piece of aluminum foil to keep it from touching bottom.) Steam about 2½ hours. Make sure water does not boil dry. Serve pudding with Light Chocolate Sauce or whipped cream.

Working time: 30 minutes
Preparation time: 3 hours
Serves 8

◆

STEAMED VEGETABLE PUDDING

This steamed pudding is a very easy and unusual dessert. Most guests do not even guess that it contains potatoes. The leftovers heat well in a microwave oven if they are covered.

1 cup sugar
1 cup raisins
1 cup flour
½ cup heavy cream, or 1 tablespoon
    shortening
1 cup peeled and grated potatoes
1 cup grated carrots
1 teaspoon cinnamon
1 teaspoon ground cloves
1 teaspoon nutmeg
1 teaspoon baking soda dissolved in ¼
    cup hot water

Hard Sauce (page 176) or flavored
    whipped cream

1. Mix pudding ingredients in a bowl and put into a 2-quart pudding mold. Place mold in a deep pot containing at least 2 inches of water. Rest mold on a piece of crumpled aluminum foil so it does not sit on bottom. Cover with aluminum foil and steam for 2 hours.

2. Serve with Hard Sauce or flavored whipped cream.

Working time: 20 minutes
Preparation time: 3 hours
Serves 6–8

◆

SHERRY TRIFLE

Perhaps the most famous of English puddings, this is an easy dish to make and tastes very good even if not made with homemade cake. You should not follow the recipe slavishly; let your imagination and sense of aesthetics have full play.

1 jelly-roll sponge cake or piece of
     homemade pound cake about 5
     inches long, 4 inches wide and
     3 inches high; or one 12-ounce
     packaged pound cake
6-ounce jar seedless raspberry
     jam mixed with 1 teaspoon
     lemon juice
2 cups heavy cream
2 tablespoons superfine sugar
2 cups fresh raspberries, or two
     10-ounce packages frozen
     raspberries, defrosted and
     thoroughly drained; or equal
     amount of other berries
1 cup blanched almonds, separated
     into halves
Double recipe of Vanilla Custard
     Sauce (page 175), chilled
     until firm
1 cup medium-dry sherry
¼ cup brandy
Fresh whole berries or nuts,
     for garnish

1. Cut half of cake into ¾-inch-thick
   slices and coat with raspberry jam,
   (unless you are using jelly roll,
   which is already filled with jam).
   Place some cake slices, jam side up,
   in bottom of a 12-inch glass serving
   bowl about 8 to 10 inches deep.
   Stick more slices to sides of bowl
   and cut remaining cake into 1-inch
   cubes and set aside.

2. In a chilled bowl, whip cream until
   it thickens slightly. Add superfine
   sugar and continue to beat until
   cream is stiff enough to form peaks.

3. Fill bowl with alternate layers of
   fruit, nuts, custard sauce, and cake
   cubes. Sprinkle layers with sherry
   and brandy. (If fruit is bitter, sprinkle with additional sugar.)

4. Spoon on some whipped cream
   and, using a pastry bag, pipe the
   rest decoratively on top. Garnish
   with a few large berries and a
   few nuts.

NOTE: The trifle will be at its best
when served at once, but it may be
refrigerated for an hour or two. The
dessert gets watery if left too long.

Working time: 30 minutes
Preparation time: 1 hour
Serves 8

◆

CHAPTER 8

SIMPLY FRUIT

Melon and Ginger Compote (page 142)

Sometimes the simplest of desserts can be the most satisfying. This is not to say that simple fruit desserts are quick to prepare; you can easily spend an hour on a good fruit mélange. Seeding grapes, pitting cherries, forming melon balls, and cutting pineapple wedges are slow and messy jobs.

Hot fruit desserts appear fancy while remaining easy to make and relatively fat free. Fruit compote, hot or cold, has endless variations and, accompanied by a buttery pound cake, is a lovely end to a rich meal.

It is increasingly difficult to find tree- or vine-ripened fruit except where it is grown. Instead, supermarkets carry a vast array of exotic fruits that left their homes as adolescents and never lived to ripe old age. These supermarket products often need the added flavor of spices and the accompaniment of pastry to make a presentable finale. Real tree-ripened fruit is so full of flavor that it is almost sacrilege to cover it with liquor, pastry, or whipped cream.

RIPENESS

Learn to distinguish the ripe fruit. It is discouraging to bring home a lovely looking melon, only to cut into it and find a hard, tasteless substance. Melons should have a slight aroma. They should give slightly at the blossom end, but be very hard everywhere else. A soft spot on the side denotes bruising.

Berries often look better than they taste. When examining out-of-season fruit that has been transported halfway around the world, look into the middle of the basket. Don't buy fruit that has spots of mold, which spreads very fast. When choosing strawberries, look at the stem end and make sure that the hulls are still fresh and green. Some berries carry a certain amount of white color, which is not necessarily a guide to flavor.

Peaches and their cousins, nectarines, are extremely difficult to choose in a market. Unless pressed for time, buy one, try it, and then decide if you want to buy more. A peach that starts out woody will never improve; it will only get mushy with age. A properly ripe one will be very juicy.

Pineapples should have a nice aroma, and should easily give up a center leaf when it is pulled. As with peaches, juice should flow when the fruit is cut. You can sometimes find pineapple in the markets that has been skinned, cored, and wrapped in plastic for convenience. While ordinarily I avoid prepared fruit, I have found that in this case it is easy to see the really juicy pineapples and to avoid the overripe, slightly off-color, or transparent ones.

Red bananas are delicious when ripe and irritating to buy. Don't bother to buy them unless you have patience. If they look nice in the store, they will generally take several weeks to ripen at home. If they look dead and black-spotted when you buy them, you will probably still need to wait a week. If the skin does not want to peel back, they are not ready. But for the determined cook, they make the best flambéed bananas.

With exotic fruit, such as kiwis, mangoes, and persimmons, there are no hard-and-fast rules. Experiment and learn to know how soft each should be.

CARE

Most supermarket fruits have been chilled during their trip from farm to market, and they will spoil quite quickly if left at room temperature. Berries should have their covers removed at once and be turned out on a plate so any damaged ones can be discarded. The berries should then be covered loosely to prevent drying out but to allow some air circulation.

Strawberries and other firm berries are cleaned by immersing in cold water or running under a faucet briefly to remove sand. They should then be turned out onto a clean dish towel and rolled around on it until dry. Raspberries must never see water; when wet, they disintegrate into a soggy mess. Since water won't remove the insecticides anyway, you might just as well enjoy them.

LEMON OR LIME

Both juice and zest of lemon are useful to add strength of taste to many fruit dishes. For fruit mixtures and sauces, for example, cooks depend on lemon to cut the sweet taste and to make the sauces more interesting. The specified quantities are merely suggestions, since lemons vary dramatically in strength of flavor and quantity of juice. Good-quality limes can often be substituted, but use less juice than specified for lemon. Lime zest tends to be more bitter than lemon zest, unless the lime is tree ripened. Key limes, which are small, round, and thin skinned, can be found in Florida and in the Caribbean. Key lime juice is wonderful, and adds to almost any fruit dish.

MELON AND GINGER COMPOTE

A refreshing fruit dessert especially for luncheon in the summer (see photograph on page 139). It is nice served with a Brownie (page 77). Buy the best possible ginger preserved in syrup, usually imported from China and sold in a green glazed pottery jar with a cork top.

2 ripe cantaloupes, Persian melons, or
  honeydew melons
½ cup preserved ginger, in syrup
½ lemon (optional)

1. Cut all usable flesh from melons into balls with a melon baller. Put scraps of melon and rinds through a sieve to make juice. Drain and cut ginger into ¼-inch dice, reserving syrup.

2. Pour ginger syrup and ginger over melon balls and chill in refrigerator for at least 1 hour. Taste and add lemon juice if melon seems too sweet.

Working time: 15 minutes
Preparation time: 1½ hours
Serves 6–8

◆

FRESH FRUIT COMPOTE

A fresh fruit compote or mélange can be an aesthetic and tasteful masterpiece, or just a bowl of fruit salad. Making a good juice and using complementary fruits is part of the key. Avoid using any fruit that you just happen to have on hand: bananas get mushy, apples distract when used with berries and melon by being too crunchy. The choice is a matter of personal preference. Experiment.

Grapes, melon balls, and strawberries is one good combination. Apples, bananas, and oranges is another possibility. Remember, however, that liqueur sometimes complements berries, but often detracts.

2 cups fresh strawberries
2 cups cantaloupe balls
2 cups seedless green grapes
2 cups pitted fresh cherries
1 cup fresh raspberries
Superfine sugar, to taste
1 tablespoon fresh lemon juice

1. Slice strawberries if large. Mix fruits in bowl you will serve them in.

2. Push all melon scraps through a coarse sieve to create juice. Create more juice by mashing and straining some raspberries, strawberries, or more melon. Add juice to bowl.

3. Add superfine sugar to taste only if very tart. A pinch of salt or several tablespoons of lemon juice may also bring out additional flavor. Frequent tasting is the key to success. Chill and serve cold.

Working time: 30 minutes
Preparation time: 50 minutes
Serves 6–8

HOT FRUIT COMPOTE

This is a good way to use fruit that has been sitting in the freezer a little too long. It tastes wonderful on a cold day, and it travels well. Without the cream it is healthful and low in fat. If you are looking for a richer dessert, serve it with cake or cookies.

To make this dessert successfully, be sure that each fruit cooks only as long as necessary. The dish can be kept warm in a chafing dish, so it is especially good for buffets.

Dried fruits (raisins, prunes, apricots)

Frozen fruits with their juice
(peaches, raspberries,
blueberries, pears)

Canned fruits with their juice
(peaches, pears, apricots)

Fresh fruits (grapes, apples, pears,
oranges, plums, and nectarines)

Grape, apple, or orange juice
(optional)

Brown sugar (optional)

Lemon juice and zest (optional)

Whole cloves (optional)

Cinnamon sticks (optional)

1 tablespoon cornstarch for every
2 cups of juice (optional)

Rum or brandy

Chopped nuts, for garnish

1. Fill a large ovenproof dish — one big enough to hold about 2 cups fruit per person to be served — with a mixture of dried fruits, frozen fruits, canned fruits, and fresh fruits, keeping aside those fruits that require shorter cooking times, such as grapes, ripe peaches, and berries. (Two cups of fruit per person will yield 1–1½ cups when cooked.)

2. Add juice from frozen or canned fruit, or add water, orange juice, or bottled grape or apple juice. Add brown sugar, if desired. Lemon juice and zest, cloves, cinnamon sticks, and so on, are good additions, too.

3. Bake in oven at 350° to 400°F., or on top of stove just until fruit is tender and very hot. Just before fruit is cooked, add reserved fruit that needs shorter cooking time.

4. If desired, drain juices and thicken. Heat in a separate pan with 1 tablespoon cornstarch mixed with equal amount of cold water per 2 cups of juice, and boil until thick enough to suit.

5. At last moment, add brandy or rum, chopped roasted almonds, or other nuts to mixture to taste. Do not reheat. Serve with cream on the side or Vanilla Custard Sauce (page 175).

Working time: 50 minutes
Preparation time: 1½ hours
Plan on ¾–1½ cups per person

◆

RASPBERRY GELATIN

Homemade gelatin bears little resemblance to the store-bought variety made with artificial ingredients. Any berry or citrus fruit juice can be used in this recipe; if fresh berries are chosen, add sugar to the hot gelatin mixture to taste. The proportions are always the same: 3 cups liquid to 1 tablespoon gelatin if you like it somewhat soft, or 1½ tablespoons gelatin for a firmer dessert.

2 10-ounce packages frozen
    raspberries, sweetened to taste
½ tablespoon unflavored gelatin
½ cup water
Juice of 1 lemon

1. Puree raspberries through a fine strainer such as a *chinois*.

2. Soften gelatin in cold water, then heat gently until dissolved.

3. Combine ingredients and chill in 6 individual molds or one 1-quart mold for several hours, or until gelatin is firm.

Working time: 10 minutes
Preparation time: 3 hours
Serves 4–6

◆

BROILED PEACHES

This dessert is best cooked at the last moment. If preparing fruit in advance for cooking, rub the peach halves with a cut lemon half to prevent discoloration. (See photograph on page 127.)

4 ripe peaches, or 8 canned peach
    halves, drained
½ cup light brown sugar, packed

3 tablespoons water
2 tablespoons butter
¼ to ⅓ cup water (optional)
½ cup sliced almonds

1. Preheat broiler to medium. Immerse peaches in boiling water for about 15 seconds, then remove and slip skin off with fingers. Cut in half, remove pits, and place hollow side up in a gratin pan or other heatproof low-sided casserole.

2. Melt brown sugar, water, and butter in a saucepan and pour over peaches. Pour an extra 2 tablespoons of water in bottom of pan if there is not sufficient sugar mixture to cover bottom.

3. Place dish in broiler and broil about 10 to 15 minutes, watching constantly to prevent burning. Peaches should be hot, caramelized, and still quite firm. When almost cooked, sprinkle with almonds and put back under broiler until almonds are toasted. Serve immediately.

Working time: 15 minutes
Preparation time: 25 minutes
Serves 4

◆

PLUM DUMPLINGS

This may be prepared partly in advance with some practice. If you must be with your guests, time it so that you put the dumplings into the already boiling water as you sit down to eat and turn the heat down low; this assumes you can come back to remove them in 10 to 15 minutes, while the dishes are being cleared. The butter can be lightly browned ahead of time, and at the last minute heated again being careful not to burn it. Add the cinnamon and sugar after the butter is browned, stir for 5 seconds, and remove from the heat. The dumplings are worth the fuss!

DUMPLINGS

½ package active dry yeast
2 cups milk, brought to a boil and
    cooled to lukewarm
1 teaspoon sugar

2 cups flour
1 tablespoon butter
3 pounds Italian or other
    freestone plums

CINNAMON SAUCE

½ **cup butter**
¼ **cup sugar**
1 **tablespoon ground cinnamon, or**
    to taste

1. Proof the yeast in ½ cup milk with the sugar until bubbly.

2. Put yeast mixture, flour, and butter in a large bowl. Add enough milk to make a soft dough, a little stiffer than biscuit dough. Cover dough and put in warm place to rise until at least doubled in height and until an impression of your finger pushed into the middle remains, about 1 hour.

3. Roll out dough to ¼-inch thickness, then cut into 4-inch squares, or just large enough to cover plums.

4. Place a plum in each square and form dough around it, pressing gently until air is worked out and an even thickness of dough surrounds each plum. Dough must make a complete and even covering on the plum, or water will get in and spoil the flavor. Dough scraps can be gathered together and rerolled. Put plums on a floured surface in a warm place to rise for about 30 minutes.

5. Make the sauce. Melt butter and cook until lightly brown.

6. Add sugar and cinnamon, and heat for several more seconds, only just long enough to melt sugar. Use immediately.

7. Bring water to boil in a very large kettle. Add the dumplings and simmer about 10 minutes. After all dumplings are in and have risen to the surface, turn the heat down slightly so the water will not boil too furiously. Test for doneness. Dough and plums must both cook, so try one before removing all. Drain briefly on a dish towel, then serve at once on a platter with sauce poured over.

Working time: 40 minutes
Preparation time: 3 hours
Serves 10

◆

PLUMS WITH
BROWN SUGAR STREUSEL

This is a wonderful family dessert. It is also great for special breakfasts. Be sure to bake at a high temperature to start, so the topping gets crisp.

This streusel can also be used as a topping for one-crust pies, coffee cake, and any fruit dessert that will be baked. It goes particularly well with apples, rhubarb, and peaches. The topping mixture keeps for two weeks in the refrigerator, or indefinitely in the freezer, so make it in quantity for later use.

STREUSEL TOPPING

1 cup light brown sugar, packed
1 cup flour
½ cup butter
1½ teaspoons cinnamon

FRUIT BASE

4 cups Italian plums
¼ cup sugar
½ teaspoon cinnamon

1. With your fingers, rub streusel ingredients together until well mixed, then clump crumbs by gripping them in a clenched fist. This makes a large, coarse, crisp crumb texture when cooked. Set aside.

2. Preheat oven to 400°F. Butter a 9-inch pie plate.

3. Remove pits from plums and cut each plum into 4 pieces. Arrange in pie plate, cut side up. Sprinkle sugar and cinnamon over fruit, then a heavy layer of streusel.

4. Bake for 25 minutes, or until fruit is cooked and crumbs are crisp and just starting to turn color. Lower oven temperature after 10 minutes if top seems to brown too quickly.

Working time: 15 minutes
Preparation time: 50 minutes
Serves 6

◆

PEARS
WITH BAR-LE-DUC

This is the easiest of fruit recipes and absolutely without equal if made with perfectly ripened Royal Riviera pears from Oregon, which are extremely juicy. Bar-le-duc is nothing more than red currants preserved in a thick syrup. It is usually imported from France, and is expensive and difficult to find. To make your own, prepare currant jelly and at the last moment, as the pan comes off the heat, add ½ cup of picked-over fresh currants to every cup of jelly. Currant jelly is an acceptable substitute, but to make it look better, turn it out of the jar and cut it up into little bits, then spoon it on. Pears will discolor when peeled, so be sure to coat all surfaces with lemon juice if they must be prepared in advance.

2 8-ounce packages cream cheese
6 small or 3 large pears, preferably
    Royal Riviera or Comice
4-ounce jar bar-le-duc or currant jelly

1. Place cream cheese in freezer while preparing pears, about 10 minutes.

2. Peel pears at last moment if possible, otherwise immerse in 1 cup water mixed with juice of 1 lemon to prevent discoloration. Cut pears in half and cut a thin slice off rounded part of each so pears will sit firmly on a plate. Remove cores with a spoon.

3. Using large side of a vegetable grater, grate cream cheese over each pear into a fluffy mound. (Do not attempt to grate cheese onto a plate and then move it onto pears, as it will collapse and look unattractive.) Handle cream cheese as little as possible so it will stay hard enough to grate.

4. Put a heaping tablespoon of bar-le-duc or currant jelly on each mound of cream cheese and serve.

Working time: 15 minutes
Preparation time: 50 minutes
Serves 6

◆

STUFFED PEARS

This simple fruit dessert is suitable for almost any occasion. To enhance the appearance for a formal dinner, surround the platter with glazed cranberries or small mounds of currant jelly. You can also surround pears with Crème Anglaise (page 174), marbleized with the following caramel syrup.

The caramel syrup is best made in a fairly heavy pan; I usually use a small frying pan and stir constantly with a wooden spoon.

To make this into a fancy dish, prepare a Short Crust Pastry shell (page 91), prebaked and lined with Cream Cheese Filling (page 193), and then place the cooked pears on top. Serve the sauce on the side.

CARAMEL SYRUP

½ cup sugar
½ cup plus 2 tablespoons water

PEARS

1½-inch piece of vanilla bean
½ cup walnut pieces
4 tablespoons butter
¼ cup bread crumbs
1 egg yolk
Pinch of black pepper
1 tablespoon honey
1 tablespoon plus 2 teaspoons sugar
3 pears, preferably Royal Riviera or
    Comice, peeled and halved
1 tablespoon pear brandy mixed with
    3 tablespoons water (optional)

1. Make the syrup. Dissolve ½ cup of sugar over low heat in 2 tablespoons water. Wipe down crystals that might form on the side of pan with a fork wrapped in a wet paper towel. Watching carefully so it doesn't burn, cook sugar until a rich caramel color. Remove from heat and, being careful not to get splattered, add remaining ½ cup hot water and stir to combine. Set aside to cool.

2. Split vanilla bean lengthwise and scrape out seeds. Mix with walnuts. Preheat oven to 350°F.

3. In a food processor, chop walnuts and vanilla seeds for about 10 seconds. Then add butter, bread crumbs, egg yolk, pepper, honey, and sugar. Mix well.

4. Remove cores from pears and cut a thin slice from rounded side of each so pears will sit flat without tipping. Put pears in an ovenproof dish, core

side up. Mound nut mixture in hollow of each pear. Dust lightly with remaining sugar and bake for 40 to 45 minutes, or until the tops are browned and the tip of a knife goes into pear easily. (Baking time will depend on variety and ripeness of pears, so watch and test often.)

5. Remove pears from dish and put on a serving plate. If desired, over high heat deglaze the pan with brandy mixture. Add caramel syrup and mix. Serve sauce under and around the pears.

Working time: 20 minutes
Preparation time: 55 minutes
Serves 3–6

◆

PEAR COULIS

Applesauce, or apple coulis, has been a standby for years. Pear Coulis is delicious and different. This coulis is simply pureed cooked fruit, sweetened if necessary. To make the coulis into sorbet, simply add more liquid and freeze. Peaches and plums can be substituted for the pears.

2 cups sugar

4 cups water

3 firm Bartlett pears, peeled and cored

½ cup Poire William or other pear-flavored liqueur

1. Cook sugar with water for 5 minutes.

2. Add pears and simmer for 10 to 15 minutes, or until just tender.

3. Let pears cool in liquid, then drain and puree.

4. Add liqueur and chill. (To make sorbet, add ½ cup poaching liquid and freeze in an ice-cream maker until just firm.)

Working time: 15 minutes
Preparation time: 1 hour
Makes 3 cups

◆

CHAPTER 9

COMBINATIONS AND MISCELLANEOUS

Chocolate Cabbage Cake (page 158)

Although these desserts do not fit into nice neat categories, they are some of the most elegant in this book. When you are interested in pulling out all the stops and really impressing your guests, produce a Chocolate Cabbage Cake. It may look difficult, but it is not so hard to master and by producing it you will have learned to make chocolate leaves, bake a sponge cake, and make a chocolate glaze suitable for many other uses — all techniques that you will use over and over again.

Balloons and their first cousins Profiteroles are fun to make. Like popovers they must end up hollow, which seems like a miracle. Making profiteroles, or cream puffs as they are sometimes called, requires an oven that can maintain an even temperature. They dislike drafts and will collapse if not cooked sufficiently to form a crust on the outside. If overcooked they will be hard and useless. When preparing standard ones, I always make a few tiny ones to stuff with curried crab or other savory fillings to serve as an appetizer.

With the ready availability of premade phyllo dough, strudels from scratch seldom appear on the table. This is a great pity, since they are truly fun to make and taste far better than any bakery product. The first time you make strudel, it seems incredible that a small handful of dough can be rolled and stretched into an unbroken transparent sheet 30 × 45 inches, with enough trimmings to fill your hand. Surely there must be some connection to the parable of the loaves and the fishes. Fillings for strudels are endless, and once you have mastered the dessert strudel, you can use the same technique to produce savory strudels with sausage and mushrooms, ham, chicken and cheese, and vegetarian mixtures.

Crêpes in all their forms are very useful. They can usually be produced without a trip to the store, which makes them dear to my heart. Once mastered, crêpes can be filled with savory fillings and used as appetizers or entrees, or as an enhancement for leftovers.

◆

TECHNIQUES

Strudel   The only difficult part of strudel-making is stretching the dough. Use a 30 × 45-inch table, for if the table is too big you will not be able to coax the dough over the edge. If it is too small, you have to cut the dough in half and make two. Put a plain cotton tablecloth or sheet on the table and sprinkle it heavily with flour and then rub the flour into the cloth evenly so the material is coated and there is no visible excess.

Place the dough in the middle of the table. Roll it out lengthwise to the table. You will have to be persistent at first, since the dough will seem determined to shrink back as fast as you roll it. After you have rolled a piece of dough to an even ¼-inch thickness, put the rolling pin away. Butter your hands, wipe off the excess, then flour your hands well. With palms down, reach under the dough and stretch it toward the sides of the table. Note: Keep your nails away or you will poke holes in the dough and ruin it; use the back of your hands, with your knuckles as a gripper with which to stretch. Each pull should be slow — no rapid motions. You must tease the dough into stretching. As soon as it reaches a table edge, leave a little seam of dough over the edge. The rest will get easier to stretch, since you have something holding the opposite end. It is possible to ask a friend to reach under and pull in the opposite direction, but if that person pokes a hole, he or she may no longer be considered a friend; I don't risk my friendships.

With persistence, pull the dough until it forms a large piece so thin you can see through it. There is no excuse for holes appearing in the early stages, but near the edges, as you are finishing, one or two may occur; don't feel suicidal. Use a scissors to trim off the dough that hangs over the edge of the table. Discard this dough, which is useless. Paint the dough with butter and fill. If there are any holes, make sure they are on the bottom side or near the center or the filling will spill out and burn.

Try it. It will take you longer to read the directions than to make the dough, and you will feel very skillful when you produce this classic dessert.

Crêpes   The pan you use for crêpes should never be used for anything else, and certainly it should never be washed. The pan should be about 8 inches in diameter, preferably copper with a tin lining, and have an almost flat profile. (The flatter the pan, the easier it is to reach under the crêpe and turn it.) Once the pan is seasoned, you should not have to add grease between crêpes. I melt 1 teaspoon of butter and 1 teaspoon of oil in the hot pan for the first batch of crêpes. Then I use a paper towel to wipe out the pan, removing most of the grease. The first crêpe absorbs the remainder of the fat, so it is discarded or sampled to make sure the batter is correct, but never served. Each crêpe should take about 1 minute to cook, 40 seconds on the first side until the surface does not look wet, then 20 seconds on the second side. The first side that touches the pan becomes the top of the crêpe.

As the crêpes are cooked, stack them neatly so they will keep each other warm and not dry out. They lose quality if held in a stack for more than half an hour, but life is full of compromises. If you must make them early, cover them loosely with foil, cut an air hole in top of the foil, and keep them in a warm oven not over 140°F.

❖
❖
❖

CHOCOLATE CABBAGE CAKE

This spectacular dessert is the invention of noted cookbook author Judith Olney. I believe she is also the first person to popularize the painting of leaves with chocolate. Not only beautiful to behold, this creation is lovely to eat and can be further enhanced by serving a fruit coulis or sorbet as an accompaniment (see photograph on page 155).

Warning: Do not leave the cabbage leaves in contact with the chocolate too long, since they will discolor the chocolate. It is also best to keep this dessert in a cool, dry place but not the refrigerator, because the chocolate will sweat if it gets too cool, and that can also discolor the chocolate.

Her recipe uses a basic chocolate cake. It can be baked and served like any other cake and is especially good frosted with Crème Chantilly (page 175). Use good-quality imported cocoa!

CHOCOLATE SPONGE CAKE

7 whole eggs
2 egg yolks
1 cup sugar
1 teaspoon vanilla extract
1 cup flour
⅔ cup imported Dutch-process cocoa
3 tablespoons butter

ASSEMBLY

1 cup heavy cream, whipped and
    sweetened
1 to 1½ pounds semisweet or
    compound chocolate, melted
    (See Note)
1 green cabbage (not Savoy) with
    outer leaves
Chocolate Glaze II (page 192)

1. First prepare cake. Preheat oven to 350°F. Grease and flour 2 equal-size ovenproof mixing bowls about 8 inches in diameter to bake the cake in.

2. Stir whole eggs, yolks, sugar, and vanilla with a whisk until blended. Place bowl over hot but not boiling water, and beat at high speed for 9 minutes, or until mixture is very thick and is quadrupled in size.

3. Sift flour with cocoa, and add carefully to egg mixture, folding it in with a rubber spatula. Add butter.

Use a hand whisk or your fingers to mix ingredients gently. Do not overmix! Pour into prepared bowls and bake for 30 to 40 minutes, or until a cake tester comes out clean.

4. Cool cakes for 5 minutes, then unmold. When totally cool, hollow out a portion from flat side of each. Crumble dug-out portions and mix with whipped cream. Refill cakes with cream and crumb mixture, and refrigerate until needed.

5. Coat backsides of 6 well-shaped cabbage leaves with melted, but only slightly warm, chocolate, by spreading with a pastry brush or spoon to within ¼ inch of the leaf's edge. Coat top sides of 4 other leaves, using only top half of leaf. You will probably need only 5 main leaves and 3 top leaves, but it is wise to have at least one extra of each size in case of breakage. Extras can be remelted for other uses.

6. Allow 1 or 2 leaves to harden flat, and drape others over small bowls or crumpled foil so they will harden in a natural-looking rounded shape. Refrigerate leaves for about 15 minutes, then remove cabbage leaves from chocolate by peeling away from stem edge first. Broken leaves can usually be used, so don't discard.

7. Coat rounded side of 1 cake with glaze. Set 3 of the best large choco-

late leaves on a large platter and place frosted cake on top, flat side up.

8. Glaze other cake, and sandwich them together to form a ball. Press small leaves on top, overlapping. Use broken bits to suggest center gathering of leaves, and anchor in place with glaze. Keep cool, but don't refrigerate.

NOTE: Have more melted chocolate ready to do a few spare leaves or to glue parts together. Leftover leaves can be recycled by melting into a small bowl to harden. When cool, wrap and store.

Compound chocolate is available from bakery supply houses. It is easier to work with than regular semisweet varieties.

Working time: 1 hour
Preparation time: 2 hours
Serves 10–12

◆

CHOCOLATE SURPRISE PACKAGE

This is a complicated, painstaking dessert to put together. But if you have patience and are good with your hands, it will not seem so difficult.

On your first attempt, you may be disappointed by having a few cracks develop in the chocolate covering. Never mind — it will still be very impressive. With practice it becomes almost easy. If you need to make repairs, use a bit of melted semisweet or *couverture* chocolate.

Double recipe of Chocolate Decorative Coating (page 201), warm
Chocolate Sponge Cake (page 159)

Rum Bavarian Cream (page 28), molded in a 2-quart bowl whose top is the same diameter as cake, well chilled

1. Spread chocolate coating on wax or parchment paper cut to the following sizes: 1 piece 5 × 17 inches, 5 pieces 7 × 8 inches. Refrigerate until firm.

2. Cover a 12- to 14-inch cardboard cake disk with foil. Center cake layer on cardboard. Unmold Bavarian Cream on top of cake.

3. Remove 5 smaller pieces of chocolate decoration from refrigerator and peel off paper backing. Lay them on clean wax paper and allow them to warm slowly. When they are sufficiently pliable, take one sheet and place it vertically against cake and Bavarian Cream. Keep a piece of wax paper between your hand and chocolate so you will not leave fingerprints. Press chocolate against cake and Bavarian Cream, allowing the warmth of your hand to mold chocolate. Make a pleat in top of chocolate sheet by sliding a finger or handle of a wooden spoon under sheet and squeezing gently, so it will fit the rounded top of dessert.

4. Repeat with remaining 4 chocolate sheets, overlapping each one on the other.

5. Next, make topknot or bow. Remove paper backing from long chocolate sheet. When it is sufficiently pliable, fold it loosely in half lengthwise. Roll strip loosely into a spiral about 4 inches wide. Place on top of dessert and, with your fingers, push parts of spiral into center, creating a folded look.

6. Refrigerate cake until 30 minutes before serving. Let stand at room temperature for about 30 minutes to facilitate slicing.

Working time: 2 hours
Preparation time: 30 hours
Serves 12

◆

BALLOONS

Although extremely high in sugar and fat, this dessert is worth every calorie. Balloons suffer if they are made ahead of time. I have found my guests to be very patient about waiting for batches to arrive at the table. Also, it is possible to cook them at the table if you are neat and have an electric deep-fryer. If you have leftover sauce, it is good on pancakes or ice cream.

CHOUX PASTRY

¼ cup butter
1 cup boiling water
1 cup flour
4 eggs
Oil for deep-frying (See Note)

BUTTERSCOTCH SAUCE

4 tablespoons butter
2 cups light brown sugar, packed
1 cup heavy cream

1. In a saucepan, combine butter and boiling water, and allow butter to melt. Return to boil, then add flour all at once while stirring vigorously. Stir over heat for 3 minutes, or until mixture forms a stiff ball and leaves sides of pan.

2. Remove pan from stove and add eggs, one at a time. Beat dough for 5 minutes. (A food processor makes this job fast and easy.) Dough may be refrigerated for up to 24 hours.

3. Heat oil to 370°F. Drop spoonfuls of dough into hot oil. They will puff up in 5 to 8 minutes. The puffs should be hollow on the inside. Each will have turned, cracked, and expanded in fat about 3 times. The fat must not be too hot, or Balloons will burn before expanding.

4. Make sauce. Boil all ingredients in a saucepan for 5 minutes.

5. Drain Balloons on paper towels. You can keep them warm for up to 10 minutes in a low oven. Serve with hot sauce on side.

N O T E : It is best to use oil that has been used once previously for frying potatoes or some other vegetable. If fresh oil is used, fry a few chunks of bread before Balloons.

Working time: 1 hour
Preparation time: 1 hour
Serves 8

◆

PROFITEROLES

These little cream puffs can be filled with chocolate mousse and topped with hot chocolate sauce to make Profiteroles au Chocolat. Made in elongated shapes, they are éclairs. Piled together and stuck with caramel, they become Croquembouche (See below).

Choux Pastry (page 163)

1. Preheat oven to 400°F.

2. Put dough through a pastry bag with large plain tip to make 1½-inch mounds about 2 inches apart on lightly greased baking sheet.

3. Bake for 30 to 35 minutes, or until puffed, brown, and hollow.

4. With a sharp knife, make a small hole in each mound's bottom. Return balls to turned-off oven and let them dry for 15 minutes. Let cool completely before filling.

Working time: 20 minutes
Preparation time: 3 hours
Serves 8

◆

CROQUEMBOUCHE

This is a spectacular centerpiece for a dessert buffet. Serve it with hot chocolate sauce on the side. Stack the cream puffs or serve them in a bowl.

2 recipes Profiteroles (see recipe above)
Chocolate Ganache (page 189)
Sugar for glazing fruit (see Glacéed Fruit, page 202)
Thin Chocolate Sauce (page 179) (optional)

1. Fill puffs with ganache, using a

pastry bag inserted in hole made in bottom of puff after it was baked.

2. Dip each puff into hot sugar and build a cone of round layers of descending size until you reach a single puff at top. Do not use too much caramel or your croquembouche will be hard to serve.

3. Do not let the croquembouche wait too long before serving. Thin Chocolate Sauce can be passed separately.

Working time: 1½ hours
Preparation time: 4 hours
Serves 15

◆

APPLE STRUDEL

Strudel making is fun. Do not be intimidated by the length of the instructions. It is amazing to take a small handful of dough and make it cover a large surface, and then to cut away and discard scraps enough to have rolled a whole second strudel. See page 157 for strudel-making techniques.

The same basic dough can be filled with cherries (recipe follows), or any of a wide variety of savory fillings. Do not use a filling that is too moist.

There are several things to remember when you set out to make strudel: (1) Before handling the dough, take off any finger rings. (2) Rub your hands with a tablespoon of butter, then flour them lightly. (3) Temperature and humidity can be a problem. A room temperature of 60° to 65° is best, with low humidity. When weather is not cooperative, a teaspoon of vinegar may be added to dough to make it more elastic. (4) If you should make a hole, gather together the dough around the hole and pinch it closed; if it is near the middle it won't show anyway.

STRUDEL PASTRY

2 cups flour

1 egg, well beaten
⅔ cup lukewarm water
1 cup plus 1 tablespoon butter, melted

FILLING

1 teaspoon cinnamon

1½ cups sugar

1 cup toasted homemade bread
    crumbs

6 Granny Smith or other firm
    apples, peeled, cored, and sliced
    very thin

1 cup raisins

1 cup slivered or sliced blanched
    almonds

Grated zest of 1 lemon

Confectioners' sugar, for garnish

1. Make pastry dough. Sift flour into bowl of a mixer or food processor. Add beaten egg, water, and 1 tablespoon melted butter. Mix until soft and smooth, and dough comes away from sides of the bowl. Cover with another bowl, and let dough rest for about 1 hour.

2. Preheat oven to 325°F. Mix cinnamon and sugar for filling.

3. Cover a table measuring about 30 × 45 inches with a thin cotton cloth — an old sheet or linen tablecloth will do. Sift flour lightly over cloth, covering all of it, and rub flour in with your hands.

4. Roll out dough on a pastry board to a rectangle of about 8 × 24 inches, then carefully transfer it to center of floured cloth. Dough must now be stretched over the backs of your hands until it is as large as the table top! Ideally it will end up transparent enough to read printing through it, and be evenly stretched all over with no holes. With one hand, steady dough; with the other, reach under it and, with knuckles up and a soft fist made, pull dough with the back of your hand, endeavoring not to stick your knuckles through it. Keep moving dough around and pull it in all directions to make it cover table and be evenly thin. At first it will be quite rubbery and keep pulling back toward the center, but as you get nearer the edge, it will begin to stay put. As you pull bits over the edge, they will stay and should be left alone until all is pulled to the table edge. As dough thins out, you must be increasingly careful of very thin spots that will inevitably appear. You must try very hard not to let a hole appear. The edge of the dough at the outside will be ragged and thicker, but that is of no concern because it will be discarded.

5. Working quickly so pastry won't dry out, paint dough with melted butter. Spread to within 2 inches of pastry edge bread crumbs, sliced apples, raisins, almonds, lemon zest, and finally sugar and cinnamon mixture.

6. Using a scissors, cut off overhanging edges of pastry. Preferably with a helper on the other end, take hold of the tablecloth and keeping it stretched as taut as possible, roll strudel up lengthwise by drawing cloth across table. When rolled into a long tube, fold ends under to keep the filling in. Transfer carefully — with the help of additional hands and 4 spatulas — to a greased baking sheet and curve into a horseshoe shape. If your oven or pan isn't long enough, cut strudel in half, but fold down each end so filling does not leak out.

7. Paint strudel all over with remaining melted butter and bake on middle rack of oven for about 45 to 60 minutes, or until a cake tester inserted through dough into an apple tells you the apple is cooked. (Some apples take much less time to cook than others.) Watch carefully, and if strudel starts to brown too quickly, lay a sheet of aluminum foil loosely over top.

8. Serve warm, dusted with confectioners' sugar.

CHERRY FILLING

1 cup toasted homemade bread
    crumbs
8 cups pitted sour cherries, drained
    if canned
2 cups sugar
2 teaspoons grated lemon zest
¾ cup finely chopped almonds

1. After buttering strudel dough, spread with bread crumbs, then cherries, sugar, lemon zest, and almonds. Roll as for Apple Strudel and bake as directed.

Working time: 1½ hours
Preparation time: 3 hours
Serves 12–15

◆

CRÊPES SUZETTE

The sauce transforms crêpes into a truly spectacular dessert. With a little practice, it is very easy. Remember to have everything handy to the chafing dish, and always be sure to have extra orange juice and butter available.

The first time you attempt this dish, cut the recipe in half and serve it for two. Making this for more than 4 people is difficult unless you content yourself with giving small helpings. I usually figure on 4 crêpes per person, but others feel that 3 are enough.

While these can be made ahead and kept warm during dinner, they are far better if cooked at the last moment. See page 157 for more crêpe-making techniques.

CRÊPES

1 cup less 2 tablespoons flour
2 eggs
1¼ cups cold milk
Pinch of salt
Pinch of sugar
2 tablespoons melted butter
Oil, for pans

SAUCE

3 oranges
6 sugar cubes
⅓ cup sugar
1½ cups butter
1 cup cognac, orange-flavored liqueur, or kirsch, to taste

1. Place flour in a food processor, followed by eggs, milk, salt, and sugar. Process until just blended, then add melted butter and pulse a few times. Let mixture stand in a cool place at least 1 hour to dispel air bubbles.

2. To save time, use two 6-inch crêpe pans. Heat both pans, and place a small amount of oil in each. Wipe out excess with a paper napkin so pans are lightly coated.

3. Pour in about 2 tablespoons of batter and tilt pan quickly in a circular motion so batter covers bottom thinly and evenly. Cook until just brown on bottom, then carefully lift crêpe with your fingers or a very flexible pointed spatula and flip. Brown other side for a few seconds. Each crêpe should take about 2 to 3 minutes at most. As they are finished, stack on a plate between layers of wax paper and keep warm. Regrease pan only if absolutely necessary.

4. Rub oranges all over with sugar lumps to extract aromatic oils from skins. Remove just orange-colored part of peel with a vegetable peeler and put it with the sugar lumps in a food processor and chop finely, or do it by hand. Set aside.

5. Squeeze orange juice and set aside. Cream butter and set aside. Mea-

sure desired amount of liqueur and set aside.

6. Heat chafing dish, which should be at least 14 inches wide and have an edge only ¾ inch high. When it is spitting hot, add ⅓ of the butter. Just as it starts to brown, add sugar; as sugar starts to caramelize, add most of orange juice and rest of butter.

7. Working very quickly, dip each crêpe in bubbling sauce, coating both sides. Fold into quarters, leaving the best looking side out, and put at side of the pan. Turn down heat if necessary. Keep dipping and folding until the pan is full. Taste sauce and adjust proportion of orange juice to butter if necessary. Be sure there is plenty of juice.

8. Sprinkle crêpes with liqueur, and carefully tip pan so the fumes ignite. Shake pan gently a few times to mix sauce and serve at once.

Working time: 1½ hours
Preparation time: 2 hours
Serves 4–6

◆

CHAPTER 10

SAUCES

Ginger Floating Island with Marbleized Raspberry Sauce (page 119) and Crème Anglaise (page 174)

❖

The French writer Voltaire claimed that, "The English have 42 religions, but only two sauces." Times have changed and good English restaurants and sauces abound. In the United States, we have sauces from many countries. It is often the sauce that makes a simple dessert elegant.

The choice of sauce can make or destroy a dish. A sauce marks the dessert with the personality of the cook. Even a simple dessert like storebought ice cream can be made special by a sauce and an attractive presentation. Because sauces are a personal preference, I will suggest guidelines, rather than directions to be followed slavishly. Experiment with taste and texture.

There are two kinds of fruit sauces. One kind is made from fresh or frozen fruit — chopped, pureed, cooked or uncooked. The other is made from preserves melted with a bit of water and often flavored with liquor. Cream sauces vary from simple whipped cream to various forms of custard.

Chocolate flavors many styles of sauces, including thick chewy fudge, thin chocolate syrup, and fluffy chocolate-flavored whipped cream. These, too, can be enhanced with other flavors, such as coffee or a fruit liqueur.

Sugar sauces vary a great deal in flavor, depending on whether they are of brown sugar, molasses, maple syrup, or burnt white sugar. These sauces often have nuts added for flavor and texture.

TECHNIQUE

Most sauces are very simple; those made with egg yolks are the only ones that need special attention. In general, these rely on the fact that yolks become thick when cooked. This thickening property gives substance to the sauce. If the yolks are heated too fast, or at too high a temperature, they will curdle — which is exactly what you want when making scrambled eggs but not when you are making a sauce.

To prevent eggs from curdling, it is safest to use a double boiler and make sure the water does not touch the bottom of the pan above it. In addition, the water should barely simmer, never boil. Most custard mixtures need to be stirred constantly while cooking; a wooden spoon or rubber spatula that gets into the crevices and scrapes the sides is better than a whisk. The cooking egg must be constantly wiped from the sides of the pan and incorporated into the liquid.

It is usually easiest to heat the milk until very hot and then add it bit by bit to the egg yolks as they are beaten. This method heats the egg yolks very evenly and shortens the time necessary to cook the custard. When all the hot milk has been added, the mixture can be returned to the double boiler if further heating is necessary.

Some cooks have a bowl of ice water handy, so if the mixture starts to "turn," they can quickly take the pot and put its bottom into the ice water to stop the eggs from cooking immediately. Alternatively, you can drop in a piece of ice and stir rapidly, which has the same effect of quickly lowering the temperature.

In most cases, custards are cooked when the mixture coats the spoon. This means that as the mixture thickens, it is thick enough to cling to the stirring spoon when it is lifted from the pan. Experience will tell you just how thick that should be, but it is usually when you can no longer see the surface of the spoon.

As a custard sauce cools, a skin may form on the top. This can be prevented by floating a small amount of butter on the surface or by placing a piece of plastic wrap directly on the sauce so no air reaches it. If you choose to ignore the problem, you can strain the sauce later or remove the skin with a spoon.

NOUVELLE SAUCE PRESENTATION

One of the trademarks of nouvelle cuisine is the elegant presentation of dishes surrounded by sauces that are marbleized. This presentation is easy to master and is impressive. Almost any two sauces can be presented in this way. Thin Chocolate Sauce and Crème Anglaise can be marbleized around the Profiteroles (page 164). Raspberry Sauce and Vanilla Custard Sauce go well around Ginger Floating Island (page 119; see photograph on page 171), Coeur à la Crème (page 24), or Raspberry Bavarian Cream Carême (page 27). The effect is best when individual servings are made, so that each diner can enjoy the design before it is disturbed. It is important that the first layer is not too thick, and that the plate is not jiggled during serving. Pass extra sauce separately.

To prepare, place one sauce on a serving plate to a depth of about ⅛ inch. Place the dessert in the middle of the sauce. Then take about 1 tablespoon of the other sauce and lay it all in one spot near the outer margin of the plate. Repeat with more spoonfuls of the second sauce all around the plate, maintaining an even spacing between spoonfuls. With a sharp knife, carefully insert the tip in the second sauce and draw it through the first sauce toward the center, producing a marbleized pattern. With practice, you can achieve many intricate patterns.

CRÈME ANGLAISE

This sauce is richer than the Vanilla Custard Sauce that follows because it is thickened with many egg yolks instead of a little cornstarch. I generally make it only if I have a good use for the leftover egg whites, such as meringues. If you do not have a vanilla bean, wait until the custard is cooked, then add 1 teaspoon vanilla extract.

2 cups milk
2 cups heavy cream
1 cup granulated sugar
1 vanilla bean
10 egg yolks

1. Heat milk, cream, and sugar in a large, heavy saucepan over low heat. Split vanilla bean lengthwise, and heat with cream until mixture reaches boiling point.

2. Whip egg yolks in a bowl, and gradually add hot cream, very slowly at first, beating continuously. When about ½ cream has been added, pour yolk mixture back into pot and cook over very low heat until custard thickens enough to coat a spoon.

3. Remove vanilla bean and scrape seeds into custard. Strain sauce through a fine sieve or process in a food processor to achieve absolute smoothness.

4. Refrigerate until well chilled, and stir before serving.

N O T E : This sauce can be nicely colored and flavored with the addition of ¼ cup framboise.

Working time: 15 minutes
Preparation time: 2 hours
Makes 5 cups

◆

VANILLA CUSTARD SAUCE

This custard sauce is served hot with desserts such as a blackberry and apple pie or fruit dumplings, or served chilled with fruit or slices of pound cake. It is somewhat thicker and more durable than Crème Anglaise.

1½ cups milk
2 teaspoons cornstarch
1 inch vanilla bean, split in half
    lengthwise; or 1½ teaspoons
    vanilla extract
1 tablespoon sugar
1 egg yolk

1. In a heavy 1- to 1½-quart saucepan, combine ¼ cup of milk with cornstarch, and stir with a whisk until cornstarch is dissolved.

2. Add remaining 1¼ cups of milk, vanilla bean, if using, and sugar. Cook over moderate heat, stirring, until sauce thickens and comes to a boil, about 3 to 4 minutes. Remove vanilla bean.

3. In a small bowl, break up egg yolk with a fork and stir in 2 or 3 tablespoons of sauce. Then whisk mixture back into remaining sauce and heat again without boiling for 1 minute, stirring constantly. Remove pan from heat, and add vanilla extract, if using.

Working time: 15 minutes
Preparation time: 15 minutes
Makes 1¾ cups

◆

CRÈME CHANTILLY

Crème Chantilly elevates almost any dessert. The name is as lovely as the substance, and conjures up images of fabulous creations served with mountains of white topping, requiring skilled hands and hours of toil. Sweetened whipped cream, on the other hand, brings to mind "dairy whipped toppings" and other such concoctions full of preservatives and air that turn to water if allowed to stand. There is much to be said for calling desserts by their French names, or using French in naming new creations.

Crème Chantilly can be used for frosting and decoration as well as a sauce. If you plan to pipe a decorative design with this mixture, add 1 or 2 packages of cream stabilizer (available at specialty baking houses) to the cream.

1½ cups heavy cream
¼ cup sifted confectioners' sugar
1 teaspoon vanilla extract (optional)

1. Beat cream until soft peaks just start to form.

2. Add confectioners' sugar and vanilla, and continue to beat until very firm peaks are formed. Refrigerate until ready to use.

Working time: 5 minutes
Preparation time: 5 minutes
Makes about 3 cups

◆

HARD SAUCE

This is a most useful sauce to serve with steamed puddings and mince pie. It is a favorite in the English kitchen.

5 tablespoons butter, at room
   temperature
1 cup sifted confectioners' sugar
1 tablespoon grated lemon zest
1 tablespoon fresh lemon juice

1. Mix ingredients by hand in a bowl, or put into a food processor and process until smooth.

2. Chill briefly, but do not serve ice cold.

N O T E : There are many variations

on this. I like using ½ confectioners' sugar and ½ granulated sugar for a slightly grainy texture. Brown sugar can also be used, and you might want to add a bit of whipped cream. Try substituting brandy or rum for the lemon juice and zest when serving with plum pudding.

Working time: 10 minutes
Preparation time: 20 minutes
Makes 1¼ cups

◆

CREAMY CHOCOLATE SAUCE

This creamy chocolate sauce does not harden like fudge sauce. It can be served on cakes and puddings, and can be layered with other sauces in the nouvelle tradition. It pairs particularly well with Raspberry Sauce (page 181) or Vanilla Custard Sauce (page 175). For variety, try adding mint, coffee, or liqueur instead of vanilla extract.

4 ounces unsweetened chocolate
1 cup sugar
1 cup heavy cream
½ teaspoon vanilla extract

1. Melt chocolate in a double boiler over hot water.

2. Add sugar and cream, and stir. Place over low direct heat and cook, stirring, for 4 to 5 minutes, or until the mixture is smooth and custardlike. Do not allow to boil.

3. Add vanilla and serve hot or at room temperature.

Working time: 10 minutes
Preparation time: 10 minutes
Makes 1½ cups

◆

LIGHT CHOCOLATE SAUCE

This cold sauce is an excellent accompaniment to the Hot Chocolate Soufflé (page 129) and Steamed Chocolate Pudding (page 136), and makes a wonderful frosting for angel food or other vanilla-flavored cakes.

1 ounce unsweetened chocolate
1 egg
1 cup sifted confectioners' sugar
1 teaspoon vanilla extract
1½ cups heavy cream

1. Melt chocolate over low heat. Remove from heat and allow to cool slightly.

2. Beat egg well, then add confectioners' sugar, vanilla, and chocolate. Chill mixture.

3. Whip cream until soft peaks form and combine with chocolate mixture just before serving.

Working time: 15 minutes
Preparation time: 1 hour
Makes 2½ cups

❖

HOT CHOCOLATE FUDGE SAUCE

Chocolate sauce over vanilla ice cream was standard Sunday lunch fare at our house during my childhood as well as my mother's. There were frequent discussions of the merits of various sauces and whether any could measure up to that made by my grandmother's cook. On some occasions, several varieties were made at the same meal, hoping to satisfy all family members. My oldest sister invented a recipe that came closest to satisfying the family, and I have since amended it further. I now realize that the cooking controls the texture more than the ingredients do.

This recipe makes a sauce that is chewy and fudgelike. If it is cooked too long, it will get chewy enough to pull out fillings. If it is cooked insufficiently, it will remain runny and appear grainy. I usually keep a scoop of ice cream handy to try it on. It should cling a bit, but not be too thick, as it thickens more on the cold ice cream. Practice makes perfect.

If reheating, add several tablespoons of hot water or it will become too thick.

2 ounces unsweetened chocolate

½ cup sugar

1 tablespoon light corn syrup

2 tablespoons heavy cream

3 tablespoons hot water

1. Melt chocolate in a double boiler over hot water.

2. Add sugar, corn syrup, cream, and hot water, stirring until smooth.

3. Continue to cook over direct heat, stirring, until mixture reaches desired thickness.

Working time: 10 minutes
Preparation time: 10 minutes
Makes ⅔ cup

◆

THIN CHOCOLATE SAUCE

This sauce is thinner and plainer than the other chocolate sauces in this chapter. It can be served hot or at room temperature, with Vanilla Custard Sauce (page 175) or slices of pound cake.

10 ounces semisweet chocolate

1½ cups water

9 tablespoons sugar

1. Put all ingredients in a heavy pan and heat, stirring, until chocolate and sugar are melted.

2. Bring to a boil and then simmer, while stirring constantly, for about 3 minutes.

Working time: 6 minutes
Preparation time: 6 minutes
Makes 2½ cups

◆

MAPLE SAUCE

The flavor of this sauce is superior to most sugar-based sauces. If you are fortunate enough to live where you can make your own maple syrup or buy it direct from a producer, it will prove a welcome use. Serve this sauce over ice cream, soufflés, custard, or plain cake.

2 cups pure maple syrup
½ cup pecans, in large pieces (optional)

1. Boil maple syrup until it has reduced by 20 to 30 percent. It should be almost as thick as butterscotch sauce. Cool to lukewarm.

2. Roast pecans on a baking sheet in a 350°F. oven until they just start to color, about 20 minutes. Add to syrup immediately before serving if desired.

Working time: 10 minutes
Preparation time: 25 minutes
Makes 1½ cups

◆

APRICOT RUM SAUCE

This sauce can be used on anything—cakes, savarins, soufflés, ice cream, or breakfast pancakes. When it is reduced and strained, it becomes an apricot glaze. Try baking sliced apples spread with this sauce until they are just tender, and serve them with Hard Sauce (page 176).

Use a brand of apricot preserves that contains big chunks of fruit. Usually the more expensive varieties are better, since they have more fruit and less sugar or added pectin. Homemade preserves are the very best, of course.

12-ounce jar apricot preserves
2 tablespoons fresh lemon juice
3 tablespoons water
1 tablespoon butter (optional)
3 tablespoons dark rum,
    preferably Myers's

1. Heat apricot preserves, lemon juice, water, and butter, if using, in a double boiler over low heat until preserves are melted and all ingredients are thoroughly mixed.

2. Bring mixture to a boil and, just before serving, add rum to taste. Do not return to heat, or much of rum flavor will be lost.

Working time: 5 minutes
Preparation time: 5 minutes
Makes ¾ cup

◆

RASPBERRY SAUCE

1 10-ounce package frozen raspberries
    in syrup, thawed

2 tablespoons raspberry liqueur, such
    as framboise (optional)

Juice of ½ lemon

1. In a blender or food processor, puree the raspberries and their syrup with the raspberry liqueur until mixture is smooth.

2. Strain mixture through a fine-meshed sieve to remove the seeds. Chill until ready to serve.

N O T E : You can also make Raspberry Sauce using 1 quart fresh raspberries, sprinkled with ½ cup sugar. Let sit for several hours, then put through a fine strainer.

Working time: 10 minutes
Preparation time: 1 hour
Makes about 1 cup

◆

SPICED WHIPPED CREAM

1 cup heavy cream
2 tablespoons superfine sugar
1 teaspoon ground cinnamon
¼ teaspoon grated nutmeg
1 tablespoon chopped candied ginger

1. Whip cream until stiff peaks form. Add other ingredients and mix gently.

Working time: 5 minutes
Preparation time: 5 minutes
Makes about 2½ cups

◆

CHAPTER 11

FROSTINGS, FILLINGS, AND GLAZES

Caramel Banana Nut Cake (page 46)

For many of us the frosting makes the cake, the cake being the excuse or vehicle by which to indulge in a dollop of creamy sweet confection. Frostings add glamour and bespeak special occasions. More practically, they prevent cakes from drying out and provide contrasts of texture and flavor.

As with sauces, cooks use fillings and frostings to give their individual stamp to an otherwise ordinary dessert. Frostings are fun to work with and provide endless decorative possibilities.

In considering which of the possibilities to use, a cook must first consider the importance of stability. On a hot day, a fluffy buttercream or other high-fat frostings will melt if left in a picnic hamper or out on a buffet table. Boiled frostings will get sugary and wilt in humidity or if they are kept in the refrigerator. Whipped-cream fillings become watery if they are not used quickly. These problems of some of the most delicious frostings explain why many bakery cakes have plain frostings, which hold up under adverse conditions.

In modern kitchens there are many ways to keep things cool or dry, so you can experiment with delicate creations without fear of failure.

TECHNIQUES

In most cases, fruit glazes are simply melted jam to which a little water or lemon juice has been added. The trick is to melt the jam slowly and cook it until syrupy. Then it can be painted on the cake or tart with a pastry brush to whatever thickness is desired. The glaze must be completely melted or lumping will occur. The dessert will look pretty only if there are no holes in the glaze, so be conscientious about covering every crevice.

Fruit fillings are sometimes used to make fancy desserts with layers of simple meringue or cake. The fillings can be mixed or layered with whipped cream, and can often be used as desserts on their own by adding a little cream.

Successful frostings depend on remembering a few tips. Crumbly cakes should first be painted with a jam glaze, which is allowed to dry before frosting. Cakes generally should be slightly warm when frosted so that the frosting won't harden too quickly, but if they are too warm the frosting will melt as it is applied. Glazed cakes can be placed in an oven briefly to make the surface glassy smooth, or spread with a wet spatula. Fondant icing should never be allowed to get warmer than tepid or it will lose its gloss.

MOUSSELINE BUTTERCREAM FROSTING

This classic frosting is very rich and incredibly smooth. Cakes decorated with it cannot be allowed to warm all the way to room temperature. If you are frosting a cake using fondant in conjunction with Mousseline Buttercream, try to find a place to store it that is about 45°F., or refrigerate it and expect the fondant to lose its shine.

4 ounces sugar

3 ounces water

5 egg yolks

½ pound butter, at room temperature

Vanilla extract, to taste (optional)

Unsweetened chocolate, melted, to taste (optional)

Instant coffee powder, to taste (optional)

1. Cook sugar and water in a heavy saucepan until it reaches thread stage (223°F.).

2. With an electric mixer, beat egg yolks. While beating continuously, add hot syrup in a slow but steady stream. Continue beating until mixture is cooled to room temperature. It should be light and airy.

3. Beat butter until smooth. Add it, a little bit at a time, to egg yolk mixture, watching so mixture does not "turn," or begin to curdle. If it starts to "turn," add a little melted butter.

4. Add vanilla, chocolate, or coffee flavoring to taste.

Working time: 40 minutes
Preparation time: 40 minutes
Makes enough to frost two 9-inch cake layers

◆

CARAMEL GLAZE

This thick glaze is excellent on white, chocolate, spice, angel food, or banana cake, such as Caramel Banana Nut Cake (page 46).

or 238°F. on a candy thermometer.

2 cups light brown sugar, packed
1 cup heavy cream
1 teaspoon vanilla extract

1. Place brown sugar and cream in a saucepan, bring to a boil, and cook until mixture reaches softball stage, or 238°F. on a candy thermometer.

2. Cool to lukewarm, then add vanilla. Beat glaze hard for a few minutes until it reaches spreading consistency, then spread on cool cake. If frosting starts to set, warm it gently for a few seconds.

Working time: 15 minutes
Preparation time: 15 minutes
Makes enough to frost 1 single-layer cake

◆

CARAMEL FROSTING

This is a sweeter and less caramel-tasting frosting than the previous glaze. It will make a high, fluffy frosting. It is excellent on banana, spice, chocolate, or white cake (see photograph on page 183).

4 tablespoons butter
¾ cup light brown sugar, packed
6 tablespoons heavy cream
2 cups sifted confectioners' sugar
1 teaspoon vanilla extract

1. Melt butter in a saucepan. Add brown sugar and melt again. Add cream and bring mixture to a vigorous boil. Boil for 1 minute, then remove from heat.

2. Using an electric mixer if possible, add confectioners' sugar while beating hard until thick. Stir in vanilla, and spread frosting on cake.

Working time: 6 minutes
Preparation time: 6 minutes
Makes enough to frost 1 single-layer cake

◆

ENTERTAINING DESSERTS

LIGHT BUTTERCREAM FROSTING

This is a lighter version of the traditional mousseline buttercream, and is somewhat easier to make. It is excellent between meringue or nut meringue layers. The famous dacquoise is nothing more than layers of nut meringue sandwiched with this mixture.

6 egg whites
1¾ cups superfine sugar
¼ teaspoon cream of tartar
1 pound sweet butter, at room
    temperature
3 ounces unsweetened chocolate,
    melted (optional)
4 tablespoons instant coffee powder
    (optional)
1 tablespoon vanilla extract (optional)

1. With an electric mixer, beat egg whites in top of a double boiler over very hot water just until peaks start to form.

2. Add sugar and cream of tartar, little by little, beating continuously until thick and a ribbon forms. The temperature will be about 105°F.

3. Remove pan from hot water, and continue to beat on high speed until mixture reaches room temperature. This will take about 20 minutes.

4. Gradually add butter and chocolate, coffee, or vanilla, as desired.

Working time: 20 minutes
Preparation time: 40 minutes
Enough to frost one 2-layer cake

◆

LEMON CURD

This mixture has many uses: as a filling for little sand tarts, spread on wheat biscuits for tea, as a filling in a layer cake, or mixed with whipped cream and served for dessert. It will keep in the refrigerator for months! Also, it is a super way of using up extra egg yolks after making meringues.

½ **cup butter**
Juice and grated zest of 4 lemons
1 cup sugar, approximately
2 whole eggs
6 egg yolks

1. Combine butter, lemon zest and juice, and sugar in a heavy saucepan and cook over low heat until syrup is just boiling.

2. Beat whole eggs and yolks in an electric mixer or food processor until foamy. While on high speed, add boiling lemon syrup. Beat another minute, then return mixture to saucepan and cook over low heat, stirring constantly or using an electric hand mixer, until it is a little thicker than hollandaise. Be careful not to let mixture get too hot or it will curdle. The cooking will take about 5 minutes.

3. Pour curd into sterilized jars and seal, or simply cool and refrigerate.

Working time: 30 minutes
Preparation time: 1 hour
Makes enough filling for 30 tartlets

◆

ITALIAN MERINGUE

This meringue is good for frosting, and can be used whether or not the finished product will be baked. It is similar to *7-Minute Boiled Icing* (page 193) and is pretty if swirled into a batch of Hungarian Frosting (page 47).

1 cup sugar
⅓ **cup water**
¼ **teaspoon cream of tartar**

2 egg whites
Flavoring of choice

1. Place sugar, water, and cream of

tartar in a saucepan and cook until temperature reaches 240°F. on a candy thermometer (thread stage).

2. Beat whites until stiff peaks form.

3. Pour hot syrup in a thin stream over whites, beating continuously. Continue beating until meringue is cool. Flavor as desired and use immediately.

Working time: 10 minutes
Preparation time: 25 minutes
Makes enough to frost 1 cake

◆

CHOCOLATE GANACHE

Ganache is a chocolate icing made of chocolate and heavy cream. This version is quite stiff and is used as a filling for layer cakes.

1½ cups heavy cream
10 ounces semisweet chocolate, in
small pieces
1 teaspoon vanilla extract

1. Put cream and chocolate in a heavy pan. Stir over medium heat until melted. Turn heat to low and, stirring continuously, cook until mixture turns very thick, like half-whipped cream or custard. Refrigerate until mixture is very cold, at least 1 hour.

2. Turn ganache into a mixing bowl and beat until soft peaks form, adding vanilla. Do not beat too long or you will find yourself with chocolate butter!

Working time: 30 minutes
Preparation time: 2 hours
Fills two 9-inch layers

◆

CLASSIC FONDANT

Fondant is used in candymaking and also to glaze cakes. I have found this glaze to be superior to most others. It keeps well in the refrigerator for several months.

8 cups sugar
¼ cup glucose or light corn syrup
Unsweetened chocolate, kirsch, framboise, or raspberry juice, for flavoring

1. Place sugar in a large, heavy pan and add enough water just to moisten it. Bring to a boil over medium heat. As always when cooking sugar, wash down the sides of pan with a wooden spoon wrapped in a damp rag. Cook sugar to soft-ball stage, 244°F., or 40°F. on the saccharometer.

2. Add glucose or corn syrup and cook for about 30 seconds. Pour mixture onto a clean marble slab that has been sprinkled with a little water.

3. Let sugar cool a little, then turn and scrape with a stiff piece of metal, such as a pastry scraper, working it until it is white, shiny, and solid. Store fondant in a tightly covered container for at least a week in the refrigerator before using.

4. When ready to use, put some fondant in top of a double boiler and heat over hot water with the desired flavoring or melted chocolate (See Note). Do not allow it to get too hot or it will lose its sheen.

N O T E : Avoid putting a cake frosted with fondant icing in the refrigerator, or it will lose its texture. If you wish to make chocolate fondant, melt 1 square of unsweetened chocolate and add fondant tablespoon by tablespoon until you get the right color and consistency.

Working time: 1 hour
Preparation time: 1 week
Makes 1 quart

◆

Opposite: Checkerboard Cake (page 50)

CHOCOLATE GLAZE I

½ cup butter, in small pieces

6 ounces semisweet or bittersweet
    chocolate, finely chopped

1 tablespoon light corn syrup

1. Melt butter and chocolate with corn syrup in top of a double boiler over barely simmering water, stirring until smooth.

2. Cool until almost set but still spreadable.

Working time: 10 minutes
Preparation time: 15 minutes
Covers one 8-inch layer

◆

CHOCOLATE GLAZE II

4 ounces semisweet chocolate

½ cup sugar

¼ cup light corn syrup

¼ cup hot water

5 tablespoons butter

1 teaspoon vanilla extract

5 tablespoons sifted confectioners'
    sugar

1. Melt chocolate, granulated sugar, corn syrup, and hot water in a pan over low heat, stirring often. The mixture should boil gently for about 3 minutes.

2. Remove from heat and stir in butter, vanilla, and enough confectioners' sugar to give glaze a nice spreading consistency.

Working time: 15 minutes
Preparation time: 20 minutes
Covers one 10–12 inch layer or two 8-inch layers

◆

SEVEN-MINUTE BOILED ICING

2 egg whites
1½ cups sugar
5 tablespoons cold water
¼ teaspoon cream of tartar
2 teaspoons light corn syrup
⅛ teaspoon salt
1 teaspoon vanilla extract

1. Put egg whites, sugar, cold water, cream of tartar, and corn syrup in top of a double boiler. Cook, beating hard by hand or with an electric hand mixer, for at least 7 minutes, or until stiff peaks form and icing is smooth and very shiny.

2. Remove pan from heat and beat until almost cool, at least 5 minutes, or until frosting reaches spreading consistency. Use immediately, before icing stiffens.

Working time: 20 minutes
Preparation time: 20 minutes
Makes enough to cover two 9-inch layers

◆

CREAM CHEESE FILLING

This is a useful filling for individual strawberry tarts, pear tarts, and similar desserts. With the addition of more confectioners' sugar, it can also be used as a frosting for banana cake, carrot cake, or cookies.

8 ounces full-fat cream cheese
2 tablespoons lemon juice (optional)
½ cup sifted confectioners' sugar
2 to 4 tablespoons light cream (optional)

1. In a food processor, mix cream cheese, lemon juice, and confectioners' sugar until smooth.

2. Add cream to bring frosting to desired consistency.

Working time: 5 minutes
Preparation time: 5 minutes
Fills one 10-inch tart or frosts one 1-layer cake

◆

CRANBERRY FILLING

Use this mixture to fill a prebaked tart shell, then cover with whipped cream or a meringue topping. It also is delicious in Sand Tarts (page 100).

---

2 12-ounce bags fresh cranberries

1¼ cups sugar

3 tablespoons cornstarch

¾ cup water

2 tablespoons fresh lemon juice

1 teaspoon grated lemon zest

¼ teaspoon cinnamon

1. Wash and drain cranberries, discarding any stems or bruised ones.

2. In a large saucepan, mix sugar and cornstarch. Stir in water, lemon juice and zest, and cinnamon. Bring to a boil and add cranberries. Cook just until about ½ of berries have popped, stirring from time to time, about 7 minutes.

3. Remove pan from heat and allow mixture to cool in pan. Chill until ready to use.

Working time: 1 hour
Preparation time: 1 hour
Makes 4 cups

◆

APRICOT GLAZE

8- to 12-ounce jar apricot jam

2 tablespoons fresh lemon juice

2 tablespoons water

1. Place ingredients in a saucepan, and stir over medium heat until they are well mixed and softened.

2. Strain through a coarse sieve. Glaze is ready to paint on a cake.

Working time: 15 minutes
Preparation time: 20 minutes
Makes enough to glaze one 10–12-inch layer

◆

CHAPTER 12

CONFECTIONS
AND
DECORATIONS

Chocolate Crinkle Cups (page 199)

These recipes are designed for the artistic streak that is in every cook. They are all fun to make and fun to serve, and they make the difference between a creation and just a dessert. Use these recipes as inspiration, and let your imagination guide you.

WORKING WITH CHOCOLATE

Experts describe chocolate in the same flowery language as is used for wine, speaking of its lilt, aroma, snap (the way it breaks), melting, and finish. I have found that it is worth experimenting with new chocolates from time to time in recipes you know well, and then sticking to a couple of brands. For unsweetened chocolate I use Baker's, which is scorned by proponents of the fancier imported varieties; I have found it to be the most "bitter," and it consistently handles well. I use Maillard Eagle Sweet, Lindt semisweet, or when the additional fat is not a problem, Cadbury's Bournville. Côte d'Or is excellent but difficult to find. For making chocolate decorations I use any good brand of *couverture* chocolate or Nestlé Semisweet Chocolate Morsels. I almost never use milk chocolate. White chocolate is more difficult to work with and often has a disconcerting yellowish cast. I find the flavor to be secondary to its handling properties.

Storing chocolate is easier than it might seem. I keep mine in a dark, cool place and find it lasts for several years. If it is exposed to the air, it will acquire a grayish bloom that is of no consequence, since the bloom disappears when the chocolate is melted. White chocolate does not keep nearly as well; it may not handle well if it is more than six months old.

Technique Never heat chocolate quickly or for too long. It should be kept under 120°F. Do not heat over simmering or boiling water, since the steam dripping back in will cause the chocolate to seize and become difficult to handle. If this occurs, add boiling water, tablespoon by tablespoon, until the chocolate can be stirred smooth. To heat chocolate to the right consistency, place a pan over very hot water and let it sit off the heat, stirring from time to time. For recipes where chocolate will be cooked, such as Chocolate Pots-de-Crème (page 18) or a chocolate sauce, you can be rather harsher in your treatment and use the microwave or direct heat.

When making decorations such as chocolate leaves, keep a bowl of very hot water and a bowl of ice water handy. You can then dip the bottom of your pan in either one to help regulate the temperature. I have found that Nestlé Semisweet Chocolate Morsels are easier to work with than some *couverture* chocolates, and are much easier to find. You should determine which variety of chocolate suits you and stick to it, because they all handle differently.

When making Chocolate Leaves (page 201) or Chocolate Crinkle Cups (page 199), be sure not to paint the chocolate too close to the edge or it will be very difficult to get the paper or leaf off when the chocolate is cool.

COOKING SUGAR

Sugar is a miracle compound that, when heated in different ways, can go through fantastic changes. Making fondant is a good education in the properties of sugar. If you heat it just a slight bit more than you should, it will seize up and be virtually impossible to work and will never have the desired smooth texture or satin sheen.

Technique To cook sugar, you need a candy thermometer or a saccharometer. If you rely on testing bits of syrup with your fingers, you will overcook it by the time the samples cool. Always cook sugar in a larger pot than you think you need, since it can boil over with great gusto, making a terrible mess and burning anyone in range. It is best to have a pot that is not too wide or the thermometer will not register accurately.

For all sugar cooking, start with a certain amount of water mixed with the sugar. Then gradually boil the water away until the sugar reaches a certain temperature. The sugar cannot reach the temperature until the concentration of sugar in the syrup reaches a given amount. A saccharometer measures the concentration of sugar in the syrup by its specific gravity. This is more accurate than watching a thermometer, which will not give a true reading unless it is quite deeply immersed in the liquid and off the bottom of the pot.

Always have a bowl of cold water handy to stop the cooking process, should it proceed too fast.

GARNISHING

This is where the imaginative cook excels. Let the pictures here and in magazines and other books guide you, but develop your own style. Learn to do it quickly and have things on hand to embellish even the plainest dessert.

Some very useful additions to your pantry are thick bars of *couverture* semisweet chocolate to shave for "curls," and candied violets and other flowers and leaves (which keep a long, long time if dry) to decorate almost anything. Whipped cream always looks pretty, but it is hard to get a thick enough consistency from commercial cream. All fresh fruit looks pretty, particularly strawberries and raspberries. Canned apricots are nice if they are drained and thoroughly dried with paper towels well ahead of time. Lightly toasted sliced almonds, chopped walnuts, green pistachios, and whole glazed pecans are pretty and lend flavor. Fresh flowers surrounding a cake are lovely, but be careful that they are not served to guests.

Flowers, shells, and the like made of decorative frosting can be pretty, but they tend to make the dessert look like it came from a commercial bakery.

Leaves and other decorations made of chocolate are lovely and can be used on any kind of cake. Meringue is more stable than whipped cream and is excellent for decorating ice-cream bombes, Baked Alaska, and one-crust pies. Use a boiled, or Italian, meringue, since it is smoother and no grains of sugar will get caught in the pastry tube; there's a recipe on page 188.

Another trick is to reserve some filling and mix it with extra whipped cream to lighten its color, then pipe the top of the dessert with it.

For best effect, you should strive for a contrast of colors and textures. A good decorative effort never fails to impress and can even salvage a poor dessert. It takes only a small amount of time invested in artistry to achieve wonderful results; besides, it's the fun part, so don't forgo it.

Caramelizing sugar is easy. Simply heat the sugar in a heavy frying pan while stirring all the time with a wooden spoon. Personal taste will dictate exactly how dark you should let it get. Be sure you have ready and near the stove a greased tin or marble surface to pour it on. Do not pour it on aluminum foil or wax paper, since it will stick.

MAKING CANDIES

Candies are included here because they are good for decoration and excellent for presentation with petits fours after dinner. Besides, they are fun to make.

◆
◆
◆

CHOCOLATE CRINKLE CUPS

hese little containers are very pretty filled with Apricot Mousse (see page 23), or any mousse or light fluffy cream mixture (see photograph on page 195). You can use milk chocolate, but in that case omit the butter.

6 ounces semisweet or compound chocolate
1 tablespoon butter

1. Melt chocolate and butter in top of a double boiler over warm water.

2. With a pastry brush, spread choco-late over insides of paper muffin cups placed in a muffin pan. Allow chocolate to harden. When hard, check evenness of coating. If there are thin spots, paint with additional warm chocolate and let harden.

3. Peel paper cups off chocolate and fill as desired.

Working time: 15 minutes
Preparation time: 1 hour
Makes 8 – 10 cups

◆

CHOCOLATE CURLS

Decorations make a dessert look professional and festive. These Chocolate Curls can be made in quantity and stored in the freezer, since they are difficult to make in hot, humid weather, but they are better used fresh.

4 ounces semisweet or compound chocolate

1. Melt chocolate in top of a double boiler over warm water until tepid. Pour chocolate on a sheet of wax paper and cover with a second sheet. Smooth it into an even, flat layer about 8 inches square.

2. Using a rolling pin, roll chocolate into a 1/16-inch-thick square. Place on a baking sheet and freeze for a few minutes.

3. Remove chocolate from the freezer and let warm for only a few minutes. Remove top sheet of wax paper and replace it loosely, then invert chocolate. Remove other sheet of wax paper. Using a knife or pizza cutter and a ruler, cut chocolate into strips about 1½ inches wide. Cut crosswise into 2½-inch pieces.

4. If possible, wear disposable plastic gloves so you do not melt chocolate or leave fingerprints. Carefully bend chocolate pieces around the handle of a wooden spoon or a ½-inch dowel. As each curl is made, slip it off dowel and store it on a wax-paper–lined cold baking sheet. Freeze if time allows.

NOTE: Chocolate will discolor if it stays in the refrigerator too long.

Working time: 30 minutes
Preparation time: 1 hour
Makes enough to decorate 2 desserts

◆

CHOCOLATE LEAVES

White chocolate is more difficult to work with, but white Chocolate Leaves make a very effective decoration on a dark chocolate dessert.

---

4 ounces semisweet *couverture* or compound chocolate, or white chocolate

Small, fresh leaves, such as camellia, gardenia, citrus, holly, and rose, with sharply marked vein structure on the bottom side

1. Melt chocolate in top of a double boiler over warm water until melted but not hot.

2. Paint bottoms of leaves with a pastry brush or a spoon. Try to make an even layer and a neat edge about ⅛ inch from edge of the leaf. Do not let chocolate reach edges, or you won't be able to remove leaves later. Allow to harden, then paint on a second coat. Refrigerate or freeze if storing for a long time.

N O T E : Although refrigerating for any length of time will discolor the chocolate, it may be worth it. If you use compound chocolate, discoloration should not be a problem.

Working time: 10 minutes
Preparation time: 20 minutes
Makes enough to decorate 2 cakes

◆

CHOCOLATE DECORATIVE COATING

Of all the chocolate mixtures I have tried, this is the easiest to work with. It is the most pliable, and can be rolled and sculpted. When gluing it together, use melted *couverture* chocolate, which is stronger and less pliable.

---

8 ounces semisweet chocolate

6 tablespoons light corn syrup

1. Put chocolate and corn syrup in top of a double boiler over hot water and melt. Do not put on stove!

2. When chocolate is melted, use chocolate to paint leaves or make shapes on paper for sculpting.

Working time: 5 minutes
Preparation time: 5 minutes
Makes enough to frost one single-layer cake

◆

GLACÉED FRUIT

Glacéed fruit is more difficult to make than it looks, since it is extremely easy to burn yourself with the very hot sugar. I use bamboo skewers to spear the fruit. You must work very quickly or the sugar will cool and harden, and not be of any use. Strawberries and grapes are the easiest fruits to glaze, because they can be gripped with pliers by the husk or stem.

Serve Glacéed Fruits the day they are made. The fruit must be at room temperature, or condensation will cause the sugar coating to melt off.

2 cups sugar

¾ cup water

1 quart fresh fruit, such as unstemmed strawberries, single grapes, or canned mandarin oranges, well dried, or walnut halves

1. Cook sugar and water in a large pan to hard-crack stage, 293°F. on a candy thermometer.

2. Dip bottom of saucepan in cold water for 3 seconds to stop cooking.

3. Immediately dip individual pieces of fruit into sugar syrup. Drain quickly, and place on lightly greased wax paper. Serve soon.

Working time: 20 minutes
Preparation time: 20 minutes
Makes 1 quart

◆

ROYAL ICING

Royal Icing is a thin white glaze, made of confectioners' sugar, egg white, and water, used for piping decorative designs or inscriptions.

1 cup sifted confectioners' sugar
½ egg white
2 to 4 tablespoons water

1. In a food processor, mix confec-tioners' sugar and egg white. Add enough water to give mixture the right consistency for your intended use. For making lines and for drawing, the icing should be quite thick. For glazing a cake, substitute lemon juice for water, and make it thick.

Working time: 5 minutes
Preparation time: 5 minutes
Makes enough to frost 1 single-layer cake

◆

MEXICAN CARAMELS

While not exactly a dessert, these caramels always form part of my dessert buffet, and they are a great favorite as a Christmas gift. Be sure not to overcook, or they will turn dark and be very hard to cut. If undercooked, they will be too soft to hold their shape.

2 cups sugar
2 cups light corn syrup
6-ounce container frozen orange juice
    concentrate

⅛ teaspoon salt
½ cup heavy cream
4 tablespoons butter

1. Boil sugar, corn syrup, orange juice

concentrate, and salt together in a large heavy pan until a candy thermometer reaches 245°F., stirring constantly to prevent burning.

2. Gradually add cream and butter, taking care that mixture never stops boiling. Boil to 250°F., stirring constantly, then pour into a greased 9-inch square pan to harden.

3. Cut into squares with scissors, and wrap at once in plastic.

N O T E : If you have time on your hands, dip these in melted semi-sweet chocolate; they are delicious.

Working time: 1 hour
Preparation time: 3 hours
Makes about 100

◆

CANDIED ORANGE PEEL

Candied Orange Peel can be used to decorate any frosting, tart, mousse, or ice cream. It is excellent served on top of fruit compote.

Peel of 1 large orange
½ cup water
2 tablespoons sugar

1. Using only orange part of peel, cut it into very fine julienne slices.

2. Blanch peel in a pan of boiling water for 1 minute. Drain and repeat blanching twice more.

3. Line a baking pan with wax paper.

4. Boil water with sugar over low heat until the sugar dissolves. Add the peel and simmer until almost no liquid remains, about 10 minutes.

5. Transfer peel to baking pan and cool completely (can be prepared up to 2 days ahead).

Working time: 20 minutes
Preparation time: 40 minutes
Makes ⅔ cup

◆

ORGANIZING
A DESSERT PARTY

Parties at which only desserts are served are fun to organize, and can give a cook much greater scope for expression than conventional dinners. If your kitchen facilities are limited, you can produce food for more people than if you are cooking a complete dinner.

I usually have about 100 guests at my Christmas dessert party and I generally prepare about 25 to 40 different recipes, depending on my time and energy. I rely quite heavily on my freezer for these occasions.

It seems inappropriate to serve hard liquor at dessert parties; we only serve champagne or ginger ale, which simplifies the bartending.

With an all-dessert party, a great deal can be done as early as 2 weeks ahead if you have freezer space. Here is an approximate schedule:

◆

2 Weeks Ahead Make fondant, which needs to ripen. Make lemon curd, Mexican Caramels (store them in an airtight box in a cool place), all bar cookies and brownies (which should be well wrapped and frozen). Steamed puddings can be cooked and frozen.

1 Week Ahead Make Apricot Rounds and cakes—such as sponge cakes, Genoise, and Savarins—and freeze without frosting. Bake Ginger and Carrot Roulades and freeze them unfilled. Bake tart bases and freeze.

3 Days Ahead Make all frozen tortes and mousses. When frozen, unmold them and wrap them very carefully so they don't pick up unwanted flavors. Make sauces—Butterscotch, Chocolate, Raspberry, Hard Sauce, Custard or Crème Anglaise, and Apricot—and store them in your refrigerator. Make Sand Tarts and store them in air-tight boxes. They taste better if they are not frozen.

2 Days Ahead   Make all meringues that will not be frozen, wrap well, and store. Start chocolate roulades, but do not fill or finish them. Make Chocolate Pots-de-Crème in minuscule glasses. They will form a slight crust but will taste fine.

1 Day Ahead   The work begins in earnest. Be sure all fruit and lots of cream and eggs are on hand. Organize table, china, linens, serving plates, and utensils. Fix flowers. Frost some of your cakes, such as Mocha Walnut Torte, chocolate cake and apricot torte, which don't suffer if they are kept for one day. Make white cupcakes for Coconut Snowballs but do not freeze or finish. Make cheesecakes and Sherry Trifle completely. Make Chocolate Leaves and other decorations. Make Baked Alaska except for the meringue coating. Make the choux paste for Balloons and store in refrigerator. Make most of the sauces you plan to serve and refrigerate.

Party Day   In order to accomplish everything, you need an early start. I usually begin about 5 A.M. Prepare the fruit for tarts but do not fill until evening. Fix a fresh fruit plate. Glacée fruit and keep in a warm, dry place. Finish frosting and filling cakes with delicate frostings, such as boiled icings and buttercreams. Decorate all desserts with whipped cream, Chocolate Leaves, or whatever decorations please you. Finish Baked Alaska except for baking — the meringue will hold in the freezer for several hours without harm, and you can bake just before serving. Chill champagne in a tub full of ice. Arrange all the desserts that will not need refrigeration on the table or buffet before your guests come, and plan where rest will go. Stop in time to get a quick rest and dress for the party. Then put on an apron and finish by decorating the frozen desserts. (If you use whipped cream it should not stay in the freezer very long.) Stuff or supervise filling of Sand Tarts and other fruit tarts, and don't forget to glaze. Heat the Savarin, glaze it, and surround it with fruit. Check that hot sauces are heating and cold sauces are ready. Turn on the deep-fat fryer if making Balloons.

We ask guests for 8:00 P.M. and serve only champagne until 9:00, then ask the guests to help themselves at the buffet. While they are serving themselves, I cook Balloons and crêpes on a porch next to the dining room. This gives me a chance to sit down, and everyone knows where to find me.

A party of this type can be made much easier by keeping down the number of desserts, and by using only desserts that can be made in advance. But I find these occasions a good chance to try new desserts and my guests expect certain desserts to reappear every year.

CONVERSION CHARTS

Weight Equivalents: Metric weights given in this chart are not exact equivalents, but have been rounded up or down slightly to make measuring easier.

AVOIRDUPOIS	METRIC
¼ oz	7 g
½ oz	15 g
1 oz	30 g
2 oz	60 g
3 oz	90 g
4 oz	115 g
5 oz	150 g
6 oz	175 g
7 oz	200 g
8 oz (½ lb)	225 g

AVOIRDUPOIS	METRIC
9 oz	250 g
10 oz	300 g
11 oz	325 g
12 oz	350 g
13 oz	375 g
14 oz	400 g
15 oz	425 g
1 lb	450 g
1 lb 2 oz	500 g
1½ lb	750 g
2 lb	900 g
2¼ lb	1 kg
3 lb	1.4 kg
4 lb	1.8 kg
4½ lb	2 kg

Length Equivalents: Metric measurements given in this chart are not exact equivalents, but have been rounded up or down slightly to make measuring easier.

INCHES/FEET	METRIC
¼ inch	5 mm

INCHES/FEET	METRIC
½ inch	1 cm
¾ inch	2 cm
1 inch	2.5 cm
2 inches	5 cm
4 inches	10 cm
8 inches	20 cm
1 foot	30 cm

Volume Equivalents: These are not exact equivalents for the American cups and spoons, but have been rounded up or down slightly to make measuring easier.

AMERICAN MEASURES	METRIC	IMPERIAL
¼ teaspoon	1.25 ml spoon	
½ teaspoon	2.5 ml spoon	
1 teaspoon	5 ml spoon	
½ tablespoon (1½ teaspoons)	7.5 ml spoon	
1 tablespoon (3 teaspoons)	15 ml spoon	
¼ cup (4 tablespoons)	60 ml	2 fl oz
⅓ cup (5 tablespoons)	75 ml	2½ fl oz
½ cup (8 tablespoons)	125 ml	4 fl oz
⅔ cup (10 tablespoons)	150 ml	5 fl oz (¼ pint)
¾ cup (12 tablespoons)	175 ml	6 fl oz
1 cup (16 tablespoons)	250 ml	8 fl oz
1¼ cups	300 ml	10 fl oz (½ pint)
1½ cups	350 ml	12 fl oz
1 pint (2 cups)	500 ml	16 fl oz
1 quart (4 cups)	1 litre	1¾ pints

Oven Temperature Equivalents

OVEN	°F	°C	GAS MARK
very cool	250–275	130–140	½–1
cool	300	150	2
warm	325	170	3
moderate	350	180	4
moderately hot	375	190	5
	400	200	6
hot	425	220	7
very hot	450	230	8
	475	250	9

Butter: Some confusion may arise over the measuring of butter and other hard fats. In the United States, butter is generally sold in a one-pound package, which contains four equal "sticks." The wrapper on each stick is marked to show tablespoons, so the cook can cut the stick according to the quantity required. The equivalent weights are:

> 1 stick = 115 g/4 oz
> 1 tablespoon = 15 g/½ oz

Eggs: American eggs are graded slightly differently than British eggs. Here are the equivalent sizes:

> extra large egg (64 g) = size 2 (65 g)
> large egg (57 g) = size 3 (60 g) or 4 (55 g)
> medium egg (50 g) = size 5 (50 g)

Flour: American all-purpose flour is milled from a mixture of hard and soft wheats, whereas British plain flour is made mainly from soft wheat. To achieve a near equivalent to American all-purpose flour, use half British plain flour and half strong bread flour.

Sugar: In the recipes in this book, if sugar is called for it is assumed to be granulated, unless otherwise specified. American granulated sugar is finer than British granulated, closer to caster sugar.

Yeast and Gelatin: Quantities of dried yeast (called active dry yeast in the United States) are usually given in number of packages. Each of these packages contains 7 g/¼ oz of yeast, which is equivalent to a scant tablespoon.

Quantities of unflavoured powdered gelatin are usually given in envelopes, each of which contains 7 g/¼ oz, which is equivalent to a scant tablespoon.

◆

INDEX

Numbers in italic indicate illustrations. Numbers in bold face indicate pages where recipes appear. Entries printed in small capitals indicate the recipes included in this book.

Photographic Prop Credits

◆

Page 19: Pots-de-Crème set courtesy Cardels, New York.
Pages 31 and 68–69: Silver trays and tea set courtesy James II Galleries, New York.
Page 35: Silver tray courtesy Alan Moss, New York. Tablecloth courtesy Vito Giallo
Antiques, New York.
Pages 83 and 109: China and glassware courtesy Bernadean Limoges, New York.

Chanticleer Press

◆

Publisher: Andrew Stewart
Senior Editor: Ann Whitman
Editor: Jane Mintzer Hoffman
Project Editor: Ann ffolliott
Editorial Assistants: Katherine Jacobs, Micaela Porta
Managing Editor: Barbara Sturman
Production: Gretchen Bailey Wohlgemuth
Project Design: Kathleen Herlihy-Paoli
Photo Editor: Tim Allan
Food Stylist: Rick Ellis
Prop Stylists: Anita Colero, Judy Singer
Recipe Tester: Anna Brandenburger

Founding Publisher: Paul Steiner